SNOWSHOEING

Brilliant winter sun on powder snow as snowshoers wander among snowy trees.

SNOWSHOEING

by
Gene Prater

THE MOUNTAINEERS
Seattle, Washington

First Printing: December, 1974
Second Printing: March, 1977

Library of Congress Card Catalog Number: 74-25258
© 1974 by The Mountaineers. All rights reserved.
719 Pike Street
Seattle, Washington 98111
Printed in the United States of America

Sketches by Richard A. Pargeter
Cover photo by Yvonne Prater: **Mt. Stuart from Table Mountain**
All other photos by the author.

FOREWORD

The Mountaineer publications have grown out of experience of its members—some written by committees pooling knowledge, some by individuals recognized by their peers as authorities on a subject. No question was raised about the authorship of a proposed book on snowshoeing: Gene Prater is recognized in the Pacific Northwest and beyond as The Expert.

For over 20 years Gene has been experimenting with equipment and techniques, his restless mind never satisfied that the best way has been found. Many of his innovations have been appropriated by commercial manufacturers for their own profit. His treks into winter backcountry are awesome, and many a lost or injured hiker or snowshoer owes his rescue to the fact that Gene was willing to take time from his own concerns and livelihood to get him out of trouble.

Although it is not usually stated so bluntly, The Mountaineers have an ulterior motive in publishing a book of this kind. It is the firm conviction of some of the Club's members that if more people could see what the hills and forests are like, in any season, that these people would be, by the very nature of the scene, convinced of the necessity for its preservation.

And, to put it baldly, the book is propaganda, in the better sense of the word. The Mountaineers want people to think, once out in the wilderness, of what they are doing and what impact their actions are going to have on the area and the enjoyment of persons coming after them. No longer is it acceptable to seize a hatchet and hack off limbs for a bough bed, although many who did so were at the time clean, reverent, and brave; foam pads are an improvement from every point of view. No longer is it acceptable to bury garbage; not only can such practice turn an area into one huge garbage pit, many modern packaging materials are, for all practical purposes, indestructible. Thought must be given to every camping practice. When the snow melts, where will the charred sticks from the campfire be? Will the discreet corner chosen for a toilet prove in spring to be the middle of a trail or a creek?

The Mountaineers would also like to hear more voices raised for plowing of parking places in the winter mountains. It somehow seems that in this day and age, when mind-boggling sums can be spent for weapons which could destroy mankind, and to pave over millions of acres in freeways, that somehow, somewhere, a little money could be diverted for the purpose of making it possible to get out in the winter hills, to recreate and refresh one's spirit for the tasks of an industrial and urban society.

On closer inspection, not all users of the winter wilderness have exactly the same needs or desires. While their needs and desires are to some extent mutually exclusive, coexistence is generally possible with a modicum of the forebearance necessary to lubricate modern society in any case. As Gene points out in the text, downhill skiers do not appreciate the kind of trail snowshoers leave across a hill; snowshoers make use of the trails snowmobiles pack on snowed-in logging roads, but deplore the racket and smell of the machines; cross-country skiers require relatively level areas of preferably unbroken snow. Generally these user groups will gravitate to that area providing them the best sport, and given sufficient parking space, will not tramp on each other's toes. Where conflicting needs are not so easily resolved, regulation and posting of trails may be the solution.

Aside from the above considerations, The Mountaineers would like to share the challenge and beauty of the outdoors in winter, as conveyed by Gene's text, in further fulfillment of the purposes so well stated in 1906:

> To explore and study the mountains, forests, and watercourses of the Northwest;
>
> To gather into permanent form the history and traditions of this region;
>
> To preserve by the encouragement of protective legislation or otherwise the natural beauty of Northwest America;
>
> To make expeditions into these regions in fulfillment of the above purposes;
>
> To encourage a spirit of good fellowship among all lovers of outdoor life.

PREFACE

"You know, if you'd swing that snowshoe around a little farther, the turn would be easier. And if your binding could be tightened so it wouldn't allow the snowshoe to flop, and if it had better traction, this hike would be a snap." Experienced snowshoers have been giving advice such as this uncounted times in recent winters. And beginners have answered that this was all new to them, and why hadn't someone told them all these things before?

With the exception of a short introduction in my earlier book, **Snowshoe Hikes**, and a few magazine articles, most information on snowshoeing equipment and technique was exchanged by word of mouth. The fact that **Snowshoe Hikes**, designed as a regional trail guide, sold across the nation, highlighted a demand for an instructional book.

Over the years I have given slide-illustrated lectures on the techniques of snowshoeing, winter camping, avalanches and equipment, and helped instruct snowshoe seminars and classes in snowshoeing. This book is basically the lecture and instructional outline expanded into book form. Although individuals employ personal flourishes and variations, I have tried to describe the common techniques as simply as possible; Dick Pargeter's illustrations save many paragraphs of descriptive material.

All commercial products are treated equally in that no trade names are used. **Snowshoe Hikes** included some do-it-yourself information on bindings, traction devices, and ice ax baskets, and some of these ideas are now in commercial production. The intent has been to objectively help the beginner choose equipment without promoting sales of a particular make. To do so would be contrary to The Mountaineers' policy and would create doubts as to the objectivity of the book. Furthermore, it is still possible that an adept and perceptive snowshoer can make himself a home workshop snowshoe as good as, if not better than, any now on the market.

Several years have passed since The Mountaineers' Literary Fund Committee suggested the book be written. Some techniques have been modified in the interim, and new equipment has appeared on the market; mainly these changes are minor—a better technique or a piece of gear which will save the snowshoer a few minutes or get him a few hundred yards farther in a given time—but none has been intentionally omitted.

Unchanged is the attraction of the winter outdoors, especially to those in an urban environment. There seems to be some part of one's soul that responds to the snowy woods and mountains. Perhaps each of us silently longs for a place that is timeless, that is lovely, to which we can return and touch and know it will be there, although everything else in our cities, jobs, and complicated society is changing.

This book may make it possible for more people to wander into areas of great avalanche hazard, although considerable space is devoted to warning against that possibility. The intent of this material is not to push snowshoers to greater heights of difficulty and danger, but to make each outing more safe and enjoyable, to help overcome problems so more people can appreciate, enjoy, and return, freshly determined to preserve the winter outdoors.

Three people in particular helped to make it possible for me to write this book: Peggy Ferber provided editorial assistance; Ward Irwin spent considerable time and effort as liaison between myself and the Mountaineers' Literary Fund Committee; and Yvonne Prater, my wife, typed many nearly illegible handwritten pages into readable text.

Best wishes from all of us for many splendid winter outings.

September, 1974   Gene Prater

CONTENTS

FOREWORD v

PREFACE vii

Section One: EQUIPMENT 1

   1. The Snowshoe 3

   2. Bindings 12

   3. Traction Devices and Balance Aids 20

   4. Clothing 26

   5. Other Equipment 31

Section Two: TECHNIQUE 37

  6. Physical Conditioning 39

  7. Walking on Snowshoes 44

  8. Mountain Snowshoeing 51

  9. Routefinding 55

10. Illness and Injury 60

11. Safety 68

12. Snow Camping............................ 77

13. Mountain Rescue 90

14. Where to Snowshoe 95

APPENDIX: EQUIPMENT CHECKLIST...102

SUGGESTED READING LIST 106

OTHER BOOKS BY THE
MOUNTAINEERS 107

Section One

EQUIPMENT

Mt. Rainier from a gap in the trees on a wooded spur of Rampart Ridge, east of Snoqualmie Pass.

Chapter 1

THE SNOWSHOE

No one knows when the first snowshoe was devised by an Indian or Eskimo, enabling him to travel over the snow and obtain game; examples date back perhaps 2500 years. Although differences among early designs were likely adaptations to terrain, each shape meeting certain conditions of the local environment, difference for its own sake was probably a consideration too, as it still is among manufacturers of snowshoes. Animals with feet adapted to over-snow travel provided examples: snowshoe hare hind feet are remarkably like beavertail snowshoes, and bobcat and lynx tracks are quite similar to bearpaw models.

Early frames were wood with animal hide for webbing, laced in patterns which developed with an overall similarity, yet individual differences. Some old snowshoes are works of art, with a very fine lacing much too fragile to walk on without real damage to the webbing. Perhaps these were "dress snowshoes," worn for show as Western cowboys wear "dress boots" in town.

Change came slowly to snowshoe design, and from 1950 to the present snowshoes can be classified in three general designs, overlapping in size and known by many names. The Yukon, or trail, is about 10 inches wide and from 36 to 62 inches in length. The greater the length, the higher the toe turns up; the shorter ones are flatter, and have a rounded tail. (The 10 x 36-inch size fits in this category more logically than among the bearpaws.) The narrow Yukons work well on mountain slopes: their long high toes ride over deep snow going up, down, or traversing, but their length and weight make them unwieldly for turning switchbacks.

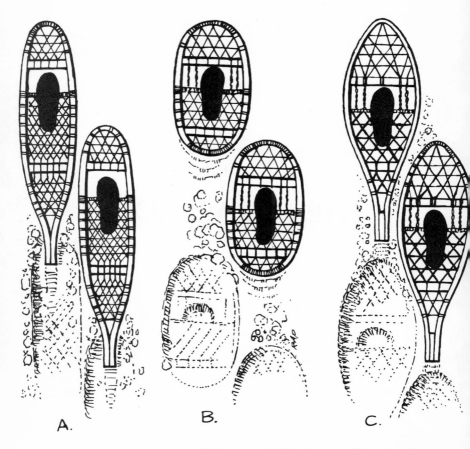

Fig. 1. Types of snowshoes: A. Yukon, or trail; B. bearpaw; C. beavertail (Maine or Michigan).

Bearpaws, as the name implies, are short and wide. Sizes range from the most common 12 x 28-inch to 12 x 24- and 14 x 30-inch. Both ends are rounded, with no turn-up at the front, allowing the toes to dig in more than any other design when descending in soft snow; longer ones may turn up slightly. Although this design forces a more spraddled-out walk than a 10-inch width, they are very light in weight and easiest to handle in some conditions, such as brush. On a traverse, by stretching a little, one bearpaw can be placed in front of the other, rather than side by side. Their width makes them much harder to "edge" into a slope, and thus they have not become as popular as the narrow designs in mountain country. They do not provide quite enough support in deep powder snow for a person over 175 pounds; one sinks deeper in the snow on small bearpaws than on a 10 x 46- inch cross-country shoe of the Yukon category.

The rounded tails of wood frame bearpaws must be protected by lacing or the wood frays and checks as it is dragged over the snow with the grain at right angle to the direction of movement. Pointed tail snowshoes, with the grain parallel to the direction of movement, wear indefinitely.

The third general category is the beavertail, also known as the Maine or Michigan design. Sizes run from 11 x 32-inch to 14 x 48-inch, with a 12 x 34- or 36-inch probably being most popular. Generally these are almost flat and have a very long tail, longer than those of the Yukons. As with bearpaws the extra width is a severe drawback on sidehills, and the natural traction seems poorer than in the other designs. Despite their extra width, beavertails do overlap, which is an aid, especially when traversing behind a trail-breaker on narrow snowshoes.

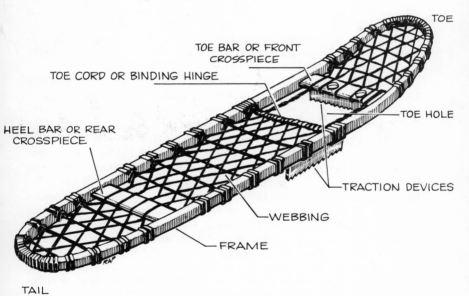

Fig. 2. Snowshoe nomenclature.

Most designs are similar in construction, with a frame, one or two crosspieces, and webbing with a heavily reinforced toe cord or binding hinge where the binding is attached (see Fig. 2). White ash, an eastern wood, is the choice of most manufacturers for frames; by steaming it can be bent without cracking, and will hold the bend for the life of the snowshoe. However, the frames should be checked for cracks when purchasing; mixed in with good quality snowshoes will be some which cost slightly less and have weak or cracked frames.

The one magnesium frame snowshoe available is heavier than any wood model. In alloy form aluminum frames are lighter and stronger than wood. But production costs are high, making aluminum frame snowshoes more expensive than wood and rawhide webs. One manufacturer's aluminum frame model, 10 x 46 inches, comes in either kit form or assembled. Strength and design seem good but many hours are necessary to lace the kits. The listed weight of over 5 pounds is surprisingly high and little saving in weight over wood and rawhide models, which are less expensive. Lacing around the rounded tails of metal frame snowshoes abrades rapidly and needs either a protective coating or periodic replacement.

One type of aluminum frame snowshoe has an epoxy-coated rawhide webbing which looks like a sheet of rawhide, with diamond-shaped holes stamped in it, laced to the frames. Weight, with binding, is 1 pound per snowshoe for the smallest size, much too fragile a unit for adults, and without reinforcement the toe cord is too weak for hiking. However, it makes an excellent snowshoe for persons weighing under 100 pounds, as its light weight and 10 x 30-inch size make it easy for small people to handle. The company has larger sizes also, but the "expanded" rawhide sheet which substitutes for lacing is not strong.

Recently another aluminum frame snowshoe has appeared on the market. A most innovative snowshoe in both design and construction, it is 8 or 9 inches wide and available in lengths from 25 to 38 inches. The shorter models have no crosspieces; the 34-inch model has one crosspiece, and the 38-inch model is the standard two-crosspiece construction. Laced webbing has been replaced by a solid sheet of neoprene-nylon which is laced to the frames. A metal hinge rod replaces the traditional multiple strands of material which form the toe cord where the binding is attached. The manufacturer uses a heavy duty binding with a deep, serrated traction device, or crampon, as part of the hinge which attaches the binding to the snowshoe. In spite of the short length, the toes turn up very high, so the tips do not run under the snow as much as the 10 x 36-inch wood frame models which have become popular in the 1970s. Although all sizes have the rounded tail of the bearpaw design, these unusually narrow webs do not quite fit in either the Yukon or bearpaw category. Acceptance of this new design has been very good in the short time it has been on the market. The narrow width, short length, excellent binding hinge and deep traction combine to create a snowshoe which performs exceptionally well on all types of terrain and snow. No doubt it is the only commercially manufactured snowshoe designed to meet mountain conditions.

The most modern material for snowshoes unfortunately suffers the most from construction and design weaknesses. Though lightweight, plastic snowshoes are too flexible, will fatigue and break with use, and sag so badly that an average size adult will sink several inches deeper than will a person on more rigid frame snowshoes. The bindings give very poor control for downhill travel, but the "greasy" plastic never balls with snow. Children who do not weigh over 100 pounds or an adult with a modest goal of a short hike through gentle meadow country can be quite satisfied with these inexpensive and colorful webs.

Raw—not tanned—cowhide is the traditional webbing material. When used in powder snow below 25°F it is almost indestructible, but in wet snow it absorbs moisture and then loses much of its strength and re- sistance to abrasion. It must be dried and re-varnished very frequently— after nearly every outing—under these conditions. If temperatures cool after a warm day rawhide freezes and develops a coating of ice, and powder does not adhere to it until it thaws again.

Neoprene-nylon is fast replacing rawhide as webbing material. Be- cause it maintains its strength in wet snow, is waterproof, and does not ball with snow as badly as rawhide, it is better suited than rawhide to the wide range of snow conditions which may be encountered in a single trip. Maintenance, except for breakage, is nil, although it will eventually stretch and sag, as does rawhide.

Nylon cord is sometimes used for webbing. Abrasion resistance of nylon is very poor, and a breakable crust will cause very rapid wear. Epoxy or some other type of protective coating must be applied frequently to prevent disastrous damage to this material.

Fig. 3. Splice for broken strap or webbing. Cut slit in ends near break, thread cord through, pull tight and tie.

Broken webbing, of either rawhide or neoprene-nylon, is spliced the same way. Several feet of strong cord, 1/8-inch in diameter, and a sharp knife should always be carried for this purpose. First, make a length- wise split in the good webbing near the broken ends. It is hard to make a neat hole with either the blade or leather punch on a pocket knife. It is very easy, however, to cut slices in straps and webbing, and with the same stroke cut more webbing and end up with the point of the leather punch or knife stuck in some part of your hand. To prevent this "great downward slash" which occurs when the point of the knife blade or punch finally makes its exit on the far side of the material, place the strap, or end of the webbing, on top of a piece of wood which the blade or punch cannot pierce, preferably as far as possible from any webbing. Even your other snowshoe frame can be used if it is wood, but metal tubing frames dull the point of the blade or punch. Press the blade down firmly and use several strokes if necessary, to make the cut. Wet rawhide has a tendency to roll over and is tricky to work with. Make the opening long enough to thread the repair cord through, pull tight and tie off.

Choosing snowshoes is really not difficult—the choices are of shape and design, and the differences are fairly easy to see. Snowshoes should be short and lightweight for maneuverability on switchback turns on slopes and in creek bottom brush. They should be narrow for security on sidehills, with good traction for climbing, especially on a crust, because even easy trails always have somewhere, it seems, a short climb or a steep sidehill. Mountain use further simplifies the choice; need to operate on slopes eliminates anything over 10 inches wide, and even narrower width is desirable.

Every snowshoe has some disadvantages. A compromise must be made when purchasing them, because no design solves all problems for all people in all places.

The action of the snowshoe tail dragging on the snow as the shoe is lifted in stepping forward is called tracking. A snowshoe with a long toe and a short light tail does not track well; the toe often catches under deep snow or crust and must be wrenched free to prevent a fall. One should be able to merely lift each foot and shove it forward, knowing that the snowshoe will follow precisely. One 10 x 36-inch model with special forward mounted toe cord tracks very well, in spite of its short length, as do the 8-inch wide, short, aluminum frame snowshoes.

Long Yukon 10 x 56-inch models track well, and their high toes seldom catch under the snow. Bearpaws do not track as well and the toes often catch. Most short wood frame snowshoes have such light tails that a relatively small weight of snow on the toe will cause it to catch, so that the tail rises rather than the toe as one steps forward.

Beavertails seem to suffer from the same design weakness as the bearpaw: the toes are too long in relation to the tail. On level trail this tendency is not too noticeable, but when climbing, traversing or descending, the wide, long toe section frequently runs under the snow and must be wrenched free to prevent a fall.

Basically traction is dependent on the webbing and cross bars biting into the snow, and some designs have better natural traction than others. The location of the toe cord in relation to the front of the snowshoe is vital. Placing the toe cord one-fourth of the length of the snowshoe from the toe improves traction by placing one's weight well forward, causing the toe to dig in deeper than on a snowshoe which supports one's weight nearer the tail. Fig. 4 shows that the forward-mounted toe cord or binding hinge causes the snowshoe to almost make its own step as one climbs a slope. On short snowshoes this has another advantage. The 10 x 36-inch standard snowshoe, for example, has such a long, nearly flat toe that it

Fig. 4. Location of toe cord in relation to front of snowshoe. **Left**, good: foot is forward, toe digs in, platform more level, traction better. **Right**, bad: foot too far back, tail digs in, platform steeply angled, increasingly question-able traction.

frequently catches, tripping the snowshoer (see Fig. 5). The forward toe cord changes the proportions of the 10 x 36-inch model so that the toe does not do this except possibly when descending. The weight of the tail section overbalances almost any load of snow the toe may gather when climbing.

Fig. 5. Effect of length of toe. **Left**, short snowshoe with long toe catches under snow easily. **Right**, very short toe.

Short flat snowshoes with the forward toe cord do have this one weak-ness. When plunge-stepping—taking long, stiff-kneed steps—downhill in soft snow, the toes dig in deeper than the tails. In this situation the toes can catch and cause a fall, especially if the snow is crusty. A 3- or 4-inch turn up of the toes minimizes or eliminates the problem.

Even on easy snowshoe hikes there is a certain amount of scrambling over or around obstructions, which is neither climbing nor sidehilling. In the real backcountry this type of travel may predominate, with in-frequent easy places. On such terrain a small, lightweight, maneuverable snowshoe with good tracking ability gives one a real advantage.

It is possible for a snowshoe to sidehill and climb better than anyone else's, yet be so heavy and cumbersome that even a short hike is exhausting. Although the trend in snowshoes has been toward small, narrow, lightweight models, some manufacturers still ignore this critical factor. As the British planned their 1953 Mt. Everest expedition, it was calculated that 1 pound on the foot was as fatiguing as 5 pounds carried on the back, primarily because the distant end of the leg is an awkward and tiring place to carry extra weight.

A 10 x 56-inch snowshoe with deluxe traction and binding weighs 6 to 7 pounds. A 10 x 36-inch model similarly equipped weighs about 4 1/2 pounds. The extra 4 pounds per pair of 10 x 56-inch snowshoes, multiplied by 5 according to the formula, is the equivalent of 20 extra pounds in the pack. Snowshoeing is tiring when compared to hiking in boots on a dry trail, and long, heavy snowshoes are exhausting unless one is conditioned to the extra weight. Small, light snowshoes, sufficient for support, will get you farther for equivalent effort.

For example, a 6-mile hike requires about 10,000 steps. Each snowshoe is lifted a couple of inches each step. If each shoe is 1 pound heavier than a comparable design, you will lift 1 pound extra each step, for a total of 10,000 more pounds than a person with lighter snowshoes. Of course this example is only theoretical, but extra weight does result in noticeable fatigue at the end of a long day.

Snowshoes may seem weightless compared to downhill skis, boots, and bindings. But when attempting to make turns on an uphill pull it is a different story, especially for the lead man breaking trail through deep, heavy snow with its extra weight on the webs. And if you are on an overnight trip and have 40 or more pounds in your pack, you will appreciate the truth of the Everest formula.

A person's weight has a definite bearing on how short a snowshoe he can use and not sink too deeply in loose snow. Short, lightweight shoes are of no advantage if they do not provide sufficient support for the snow conditions encountered. As a rough guide, a person weighing 200 pounds or more, without pack, will need a 10 x 56-inch snowshoe; from 175 to 200 pounds, a 10 x 46-inch snowshoe; from 150 to 175 pounds no smaller than 10 x 36-inch; under 150 pounds there are choices of 10 x 30-inches, 12 x 28-inches, and others shorter than 36 inches. These figures are based on my own experience. However, the new small aluminum frame snowshoes have added a new dimension to the total picture: their advantages of light weight and maneuverability encourage some 200-pound snowshoers to use 8 x 25-inch models recommended for persons under 100 pounds because their superior handling qualities on steep terrain seem to outweigh the disadvantages of sinking deeper in the snow.

When buying bare snowshoes, note that the 10 x 36, which weighs about 2 1/2 pounds without bindings or traction, will weigh 4 1/2 pounds with the necessary additions—hinge, traction, and binding. Inexperienced snowshoers on their first jaunt—and sometimes children—can be observed wrestling monstrously large snowshoes. They may well have an unpleasant experience and avoid winter outings in the future. Match each person's proportions to the length and weight of the shoes.

Some people question whether a 36-inch-long snowshoe will provide enough area of support compared to a 56-inch-long Yukon. For comparison, lay different snowshoes on top of the 56-incher. The 10 x 46 differs mainly in that the toe is shorter. The 10 x 36 has in addition to the shorter toe, a shorter, but wider, tail. The actual loss of surface is small, mainly in the high part of the Yukon toe, which doesn't normally carry any weight, and in the long, narrow tail. Unless you weigh over 200 pounds, don't be afraid of sinking out of sight if you choose 36-inch-long snowshoes rather than the 56-inch.

Rather than imply that my choice of snowshoes, and my choice of compromises, is best, I must explain that I no longer use any commercially manufactured snowshoe or binding. For a season or so I used a modified 10 x 36-inch shoe. A similar showshoe and binding, with a forward metal binding hinge and traction is now being sold and is proving quite popular. The two pairs of snowshoes I currently use and which I made at home, are 7 1/2 x 36-inches and 7 1/2 x 30-inches respectively. Snow conditions determine which pair is used. The frames, which have short, pointed tails, are aluminum tubing with a sheet of lightweight neoprene-nylon fabric for lacing, or decking, laced to them. Metal hinge rods, lightweight fabric bindings, and T-traction devices under the bindings complete the assembly.

The best snowshoes currently available still have weaknesses, but are a vast improvement over the G.I. equipment I started with. It would appear that the present add-on engineering in snowshoes is reaching the point of diminishing returns and perhaps it would be more profitable to explore parallel paths to resolve some of the compromises traditional equipment forces on users. Although most present equipment is far superior to what was available in 1950, and the limits of snowshoes on slopes have been expanded dramatically, there are still many possibilities for improvement. Some day someone is going to get it all together, and then our 1970s equipment will be comparable to the Spirit of St. Louis, hanging in the Smithsonian, as jet aircraft flit by overhead.

Chapter 2

BINDINGS

    The second vital part of the basic snowshoe package is the binding, which must make a positive connection between the foot and the snowshoe. To allow comfortable walking the binding must hinge freely, the heel rising as the boot toe goes into the toe hole. Any restriction on the hinging movement will limit a comfortable stride. If the binding or boot hits the side of the toe hole or catches on the toe bar, it may cause the snowshoe toe to dig in and trip the wearer. The binding should be easily adjustable so that any such problems can be quickly remedied.

    The binding should strictly limit the hinging action to up and down motion, gripping the boot tightly so there is practically no lateral movement. When the foot turns left or right, the snowshoe should turn precisely

Fig. 6. Binding should hinge freely up and down, toe of boot fitting through toe hole in snowshoe.

the same way, with preferably less than an inch of sideways movement at the boot heel. When the snowshoe responds this positively, it is possible to move confidently through rough terrain without tripping on obstacles or slipping on sidehills.

Another requirement of the binding is that it grip the boot firmly to keep it from slipping forward, particularly when descending. If the boot slides forward, the heel strap can drop off the heel and let the boot slip backwards out of the binding on the next step, or the boot toe will ride up on the toe bar, depressing the toe of the snowshoe and causing it to catch.

Loose bindings are bad enough when it is necessary to visually check to see which way the snowshoes are pointed before taking the next step, but if your boot slips out of the binding, your enjoyment of the winter scene is going to suffer from the interruption of putting the webs back on again and again.

Frequently there are not enough holes in the binding straps to tighten them properly, especially for persons with small feet. Use the leather punch on the pocket knife—carefully—to make additional holes. It is possible to make the "great downward slash" described in Chapter 1 with the punch, too.

Place the strap on wood backing, press the punch down firmly and twirl it around until it has cut through the fibers and starts making a hole in the wood. This is the point at which to use the greatest care and patience. Pull the strap up a little above the piece of wood, but only very gently, as it is easy to jerk the material up on the leather punch and do damage equal to the "great downward slash." Keep twirling the punch until the hole is as large as necessary (see Fig. 7). Make as many holes as needed for proper strap adjustment.

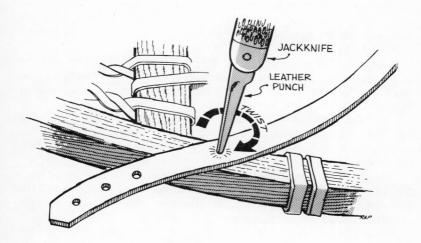

JACKKNIFE

LEATHER PUNCH

TWIST

Fig. 7. To punch new holes safely, use a wooden backing.

A broken binding strap can be repaired with cord as described in Chapter 1, or without repair cord by splicing the separated end through the splits as shown in Fig. 8.

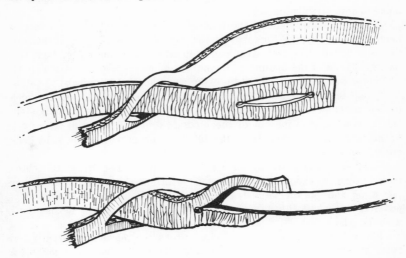

Fig. 8. Splicing a broken strap. **Above**, slip split end of severed section, right, onto other piece. **Below**, slip loose end of severed section through hole in end of other piece and pull tight.

Expertise at tightening the bindings on the snowshoe must be developed. To check for slack in the binding-to-snowshoe attachment, wiggle the binding back and forth before strapping them to your boots. This is the time—before you are on the trail—to do the adjusting. No matter how firmly the binding is buckled to the boot it will not work properly if there is slack in the attachment to the snowshoe.

First, the binding must be kept tight on the toe cord or binding hinge of the snowshoe. Straps wear and stretch, periodically developing slack. Work the slack out of the straps which hold the binding to the toe cord before strapping in the boots.

On some models thongs must be tightened; on some the slack in the heel strap is pulled through the leather of the binding. One requires removal of a rivet from a strap, tightening the strap and re-riveting it on the binding, which may be difficult to do on the trail.

There are different methods for tightening the binding to the boot. Not all bindings are the same, but the common requirement is that the heel strap must be tight or it will fall off the boot heel and allow the boot to slip backwards out of the binding.

Some bindings (see Figs. 9, 10, and 11) can be set so that the toe adjustment, once made, need not be changed, but the first time they are put on, everything must be opened up and adjusted. (The types shown in

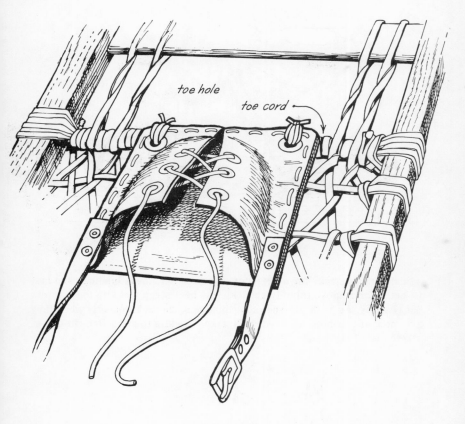

toe hole

toe cord

Fig. 9. Binding.

Figures 10 and 11 may need slight adjustment with each use.) Set the boot in the binding with the snowshoe toe cord under the front of the ball of the foot. To check that the boot toe doesn't touch the toe bar or either side of the toe hole, lift the boot heel as in walking so that the boot enters the toe hole. Tighten the laces or strap over the boot toe, then tighten the heel strap, which forces the boot more firmly against the front of the binding. Balance the tightness of the toe adjustment against the tightness of the heel strap to prevent the boot from sliding forward and catching on the toe bar as the binding laces or straps stretch. If the boot is working too far forward, tighten the toe adjustment to force it back. If the reverse is the problem, tighten the heel strap to move the boot forward.

With the pre-set toe adjustment, merely slip the boot toe into the bindings, raise the heel strap up on the heel and tighten. The initial

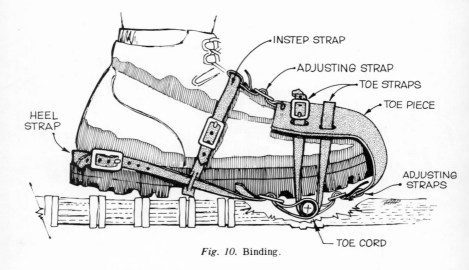

Fig. 10. Binding.

adjustment is tricky for a beginner, but once set, these bindings are fast to put on or remove (simply unbuckle the heel strap and slip the boot out backwards). As with all snowshoe bindings, check frequently when they are new and tighten as needed. It takes a while to get a firm fit due to stretching of straps.

Fig. 11. Binding.

The binding shown in Fig. 12 has no means such as the above types to trap the boot and prevent it from slipping forward too far. Though put on as described, it may be necessary to tighten them more frequently, because the binding must hold the boot from sliding forward by its own pressure on the boot at about the ball of the foot. The theory is that as the front strap of the binding is tightened, the boot is wedged firmly in the binding, preventing it from sliding forward, and the heel strap is tightened to prevent the boot from slipping backwards.

Fig. 12. Binding

In practice the boot usually acts as a wedge and has enough mechanical advantage to work forward, especially when descending, and the toe adjustment will require periodic tightening. A little ingenuity can improve the performance of these old standard bindings. Another thong or strap can be added to limit the forward slippage of the boot. Tie the cord, or attach the strap, to the snowshoe toe cord so it lies in the groove between boot sole and uppers. Adjust it so the boot cannot slip forward past the desired location, and tie or buckle it securely. Hard toe mountaineering boots are best in these bindings; soft rubber footgear does not work well except on level terrain.

The binding shown in Fig. 13 is designed to be tightened by the toe strap, with the heel strap adjusted for boot location in the binding. Be sure to force the boot firmly back against the heel strap while tightening the front part of the binding. It is helpful to place the ice ax shaft in the toe hole and pry against the boot toe to make sure there is no slack in the heel strap.

It is possible to get a two-handed grip on the toe strap and really reef on it, because pulling up is the best position for mechanical advantage. In fact, you can pull hard enough to not only get the slack out of the straps, but so hard you cut off the circulation in your feet, and perhaps rip out a rivet or two as well. By contrast, the other bindings rely on the heel strap for the final tightening, and unfortunately there is seldom enough strap to afford a good grip. Furthermore it is almost impossible to pull very hard when reaching around in back of your heel to do this very important final tightening.

Fig. 13. Binding.

A few common problems may appear in spite of these somewhat detailed descriptions. Heel straps have a way of slipping off boots although they seem quite tight; sometimes there just isn't anything to prevent a strap from working down off the heel. Ski boots used to have deep grooves for holding cables on the heel, and most mountaineering boots have a generous groove between heel and upper. But when overboots are worn, this groove may be covered. When necessary, add a strap or cord to hold the heel strap in place. Usually the cord can be tied to the heel strap on either side, and then tied on top of the boot laces.

There are numerous "home workshop special" variations of these basic designs, some of which perform as well as, or better than, any commercial model available. Some commercial bindings have definite weaknesses, but by observing how they work it may be possible to modify or adapt them and keep up with companions having the most expensive models.

Soft boots not only make it difficult to control the snowshoe, but if the bindings are strapped on tightly to improve control, the feet may be bruised or blistered. Sturdy bindings and a firm mountaineering boot are the best combination. The trend in footgear for snowshoeing is toward hard toed boots, especially double boots designed for cold temperatures at high elevations. This type of footgear makes it possible to tighten the straps or laces enough to eliminate the slack in adjustment and get all the performance the binding is capable of.

Besides taking extra time, a loose binding forces you to move carefully, is tiring to use, and causes needless falls. The purpose of being out in the hills is to see, smell, and experience the beauty of winter, rather than to study the deficiencies of snowshoe bindings.

Chapter 3

TRACTION DEVICES AND BALANCE AIDS

A real landmark for the two of us who purchased Yukons in December 1950 was a four-day trip up Ingalls Creek to Mt. Stuart, the 9418-foot peak dominating central Washington's mountains. Conditions for snowshoeing were good, with the exception of the icy depressions under each tree where the drip of melting snow off the branches had refrozen. Our new "guaranteed-not-to-sag" snowshoes didn't bite into the ice at all and we slipped considerably, but quick sprints created enough momentum to effectively cross these minor difficulties. Early in the trip, however, it was obvious that one section of hard snow would be sufficient to seriously hamper progress up the trail.

Also in the area was a trapper, whose boot imprint, with criss-cross webbing under it, showed clearly in each snowshoe track. His rawhide webbing sagged badly but provided excellent, if temporary, traction in the process. This certainly wasn't a satisfactory solution, as sagging rawhide soon breaks, but did indicate that a small area which could bite into hard snow prevented the slipping and sliding we were experiencing without extra traction.

Thus began a lengthy trial and error process of bolting, lacing, and tying different types of rough and sharp edged objects so they would protrude below the bottom of the snowshoe and bite into hard snow. Small pieces of aluminum angles were attached to the frames at different curves and angles. Rope and rawhide were wrapped around the frames. Knotted rope was attached to the webbing under the boot. Although these modifications helped, they were not enough.

For a while a 6-inch long piece of aluminum angle bolted to the toe bar and another to the outside frame were "standard." (If placed on the inside frame they dragged on the toe of the opposite snowshoe at each step, severely gouging the frame and webbing.) These angles worked effectively except for one problem: walking is more comfortable and efficient if the foot, and especially the ball of the foot, can be placed directly on top of any slightly higher point in a trail for the greatest traction. The traction angle on the toe bar is about 6 inches in front of the ball of the foot, and must be placed where it will get the best grip. In places with tricky footing—crossing a stream on icy stepping stones or a slippery footlog—it was obvious that the traction should be directly under the foot so that the entire body weight would force the device to bite into the ice or hard crust. Not only did this positioning of the traction prove more comfortable and efficient, it was thus possible to use a smaller and lighter device than one placed on the toe bar or frame.

The traction must be effective in all directions so it will hold when going straight up or down, traversing or angling uphill. A single straight bar is useless when sidehilling; on a hard crust it will act like a sled runner, speeding one down the hill.

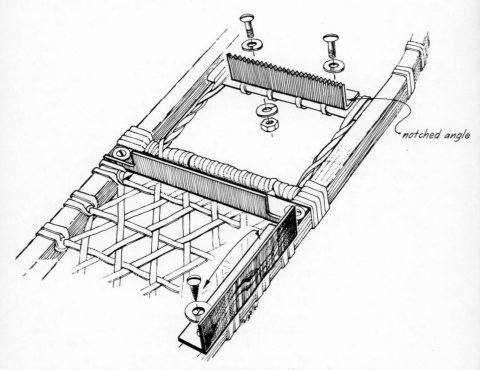

notched angle

Fig. 14. Traditional home workshop traction installed on frame and toe bar. (Not all of these pieces are necessary at once.)

The present traction devices are among the greatest aids to snow-shoeing on varied terrain. The unmodified snowshoe performs comfortably on a very low limit of slope and there seems to be a steep and/or icy spot on every trip, regardless of how short or easy it is supposed to be. Tensed up, edging the snowshoes mightily, bent forward from the waist with hands extended to catch yourself when—not if—you slip, you will soon be too tired to proceed. The energy drain from tension is tremendous. It is acceptable to be tired after covering a lot of miles, but not to become totally exhausted on a short, steep pitch because of insufficient traction. Nor is it acceptable to slow a group down continuously while someone is helped over hard parts, although it is proper and virtuous of the strong and well-equipped not to walk off and leave the weak and inexperienced party member ineffectively floundering on an icy patch like a bug sprayed with insecticide.

It is possible to move comfortably and confidently across fairly steep hillsides on dry ground. Good traction from a positive and secure traction device makes it possible to snowshoe slopes comparable to ones hiked in summer.

A beginner's tendency will probably be to shop for snowshoes and get the goodies such as traction later, to take a few hikes and see what works best and then get that item. This is sensible in a way, but overlooks one point: the less skill one has, the greater his need for extra traction. With experience one can forsee rough spots and place the snowshoes in such a way that they will hold; an expert in good physical condition can do amazing things with poor equipment. On the other hand, a beginner on the best of modern snowshoes and traction devices can make the old timer with rope wrapped on his frames look very old indeed. It is fairly simple to buy aluminum angle stock in a hardware store, get a few 1/4-inch aluminum bolts and create your own traction devices, and attach them to your snowshoes. At present only one manufacturer installs traction on his snowshoes at the factory. However, there are several accessory products on the market.

One type is a straight bar with great scallops which bolts to the webbing. It has excellent fore and aft grip, but little or no side traction. Another company manufactures a V attached to stiff material, which is tied to the webbing. Still another has a notched straight angle which may be used to form the old combination bolted-on toe bar and frame. It also can be bolted to the webbing in a T or V or in your own pattern. Or as suggested, you can buy your own aluminum and do the whole thing yourself. You might surprise everyone and devise something better than anything developed so far.

There are two drawbacks to metal traction devices. The first is the hazard of gouging the opposite snowshoe, as you occasionally drag one over the side of the other one. Keep the device narrow and locate it toward the "outside" of each snowshoe; in other words, the right side of the right web and the left side of the left web.

The second is a real problem when the temperature is near or above

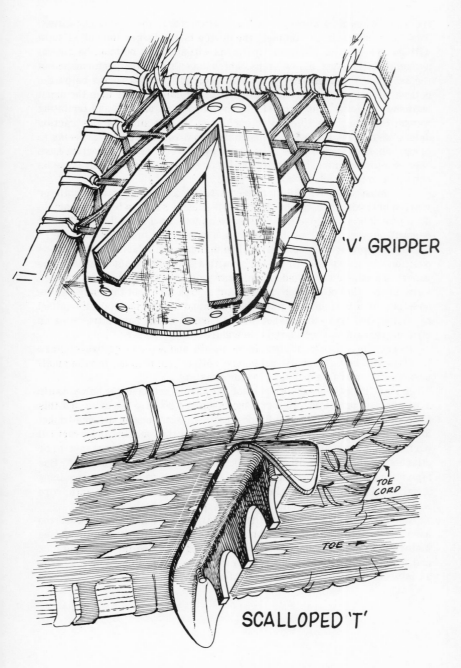

Fig. 15. Two types of commercially manufactured traction devices.

freezing. When it is warm, snow freezes to metal in incredible quantities. The more enclosed, or complex, the device is, the larger the gob of snow will be. The T and triangular patterns will attract a buildup the size of a man's fist in just a few steps, which doesn't hurt the performance of the traction; the frozen clod will protrude 3 or 4 inches below the bottom of the snowshoe and leave a trail of holes rather than the usual snowshoe tracks. The problem is the pounds of useless and irritating weight that must be lifted with each step. In this situation the traction device should be removed, if possible. However the problem seems to occur when everyone else is in a hurry. Several types of coating have been suggested, including spray-on-teflon and ski base wax, but these do not seem to be effective.

The most effective solution seems to be a piece of tough plastic or vinyl fabric attached to the traction. It doesn't seem to be necessary to do a neat job, as a loose fit sheds snow as well as a smooth one. Contact cement, rivets, bolts, or baling wire can be used to hold it in place.

Another piece of equipment vital to maintaining balance in precarious positions is a ski pole or an ice ax with a ski pole basket attached. The expert snowshoer can stand on one snowshoe on a steep slope and grace-fully swing the other web around for a kick turn, but this may be im-possible for a beginner. For both beginner and expert, the stability gained by using ice ax with basket or ski poles means easier traveling on difficult terrain and less fatigue to endure.

Heavy duty poles, adjustable in length and with large baskets, are the type to buy. Downhill poles are better than nothing, but the small baskets sink much deeper than larger ones.

A good many snowshoers do not ski and do not have ski poles. Quite a number of mountain climbers snowshoe and so have ice axes, but this tool was of no use in deep soft snow until someone bought a large basket for a G.I. ski pole and attached it to his ice ax, thus making it a practical part of a snowshoer's equipment. Ice ax baskets are now designed to be attached to the ice ax without drilling holes, which weaken the shaft. One type uses a radiator hose-style clamp to tighten it to the shaft, requiring a screwdriver for installation or removal. Another has an elastic cord which hooks on the glide ring stop and requires no tools at all.

During very cold weather, the metal ice ax head tends to chill the hand. A solution is to cement 1/8-inch thick ensolite, an insulating material similar to foam rubber, on the head. Leaving the tip of the pick and adze uncovered makes the covering less likely to peel off when the ax is used to chop steps or level the tent platform.

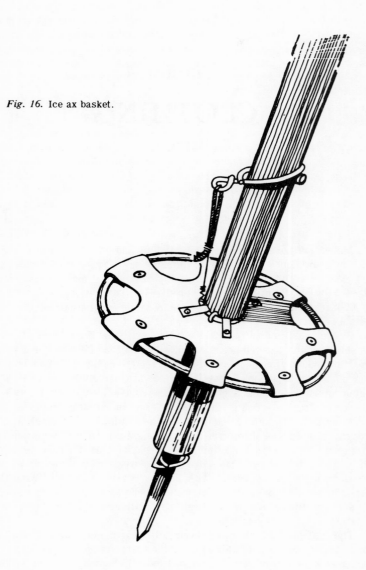

Fig. 16. Ice ax basket.

Chapter 4
CLOTHING

Mountains have great variation of slope and snow conditions, and just as the snowshoe best adapted to the most varied conditions is the one to get, so must clothing be chosen. In the Cascades it may be a warm 30°F to 40°F on Mt. Rainier between Paradise at 5500 feet and Camp Muir at 10,000 feet, while the wind blows across the crater rim at 14,410 feet with a temperature of -5°F.

By contrast subzero arctic air can settle in the valleys of eastern Washington and the temperature may be -25°F at 1700 feet. Fifty miles west at 3000-foot Snoqualmie Pass in the Cascades it may be only 0°F, and on top of 5500-foot Denny Peak, a comparatively balmy 25°F. These temperature inversions are common and contradict the general rule that the temperature drops 3°F for each 1000 feet of elevation gain.

A system of clothing should be devised which is adaptable to these extremes of temperature, yet light in weight and requiring only minutes to adjust. The exertion of climbing or breaking trail through deep, loose snow generates sweat. Moisture, from sweat or melting snow, is the greatest problem connected with keeping warm in winter. Wool is the common choice for shirt, pants, mitts, socks and cap, as it is composed of springy fibers which, although wet, will retain trapped air, the insulating factor in any garment.

The warmest of clothing, down-filled garments, must be kept dry; they easily become wet, which forces the trapped air out. The water then becomes a conductor, drawing warmth from the body. Cotton and synthetic fibers trap much less air than lightweight down or heavy wool, making them poor choices for shirt and pants, as it is certain that some sweating will occur. An improved polyester batting has recently been developed which is nearly equal to down in warmth when compared by loft or volume of material. It is composed of springy fibers which do not mat when wet as does down, thus retaining insulating value even when wet. Its weight is greater than down, but cost is less. These advantages make it worth consideration when purchasing a cold weather insulated parka.

The greatest deficiency of wool clothing is its permeability to wind. A breeze will blow right through it, and when you arrive on a ridgetop, sweaty from the ascent, wind will be noticed immediately. For this problem, shell clothing will give good protection. Wind parka with hood and pockets, and wind pants, both large and loose, should be of a tightly woven cloth but preferably not coated, as coatings are usually water-proof and hold sweat inside. (Coated fabrics have severe drawbacks, including the tendency of the coating to peel off with age.) The wind parka should be loose, so it will go on over the down jacket, and water repellent to protect it from moisture, such as blowing or falling snow.

Shell clothing can be slipped on quickly, especially if your snowshoes have bindings which are easy to remove. Otherwise get full length zip-pers in the wind pants so they may be put on without removing the snow-shoes. By cutting heat loss due to wind, the windbreakers will be equal in insulating value to long underwear or a light jacket and weigh much less.

Protect the hands, as they are easily frostbitten and almost every-thing you handle in winter has snow on it. Overmitts are as important to wool mitts as wind parka and pants are to shirt and pants. Overmitts should be nearly waterproof on the hand, with gauntlets reaching up on the forearm. Carry extra wool mitts—Indian knits are excellent—especially when camping overnight. Down mitts are good for extremely cold tem-peratures, especially with wool mitts inside, to cover cold seams where there is no down insulation, or when gripping a cold ice ax head tightly.

The down or thick polyester jacket is a must for all winter outings, and ski warm up pants should be substituted for wind pants if really cold weather or severe wind is expected. The warm ups should have full-length zippers, so they can be put on without removing snowshoes. This is a real time saver, as occasionally you want to get them on quickly. Suspenders or a belt should be used to keep these overpants up. If the pants crotch sags extra effort is needed to step forward. Snowshoes require enough effort without any extra from low-slung trousers.

It is important to have good head gear, as heat loss from the un-covered head may be equal to the entire body heat production when at rest. The cap should be a combination face mask and stocking cap, large enough to pull down over the ears, or down to the neck when the weather is bad. Most face masks have eye holes, a nose hole and a mouth hole. Better is one with a wide opening which can expose the face from eye-brows to chin, or be closed to cover mouth and nose, with goggles to protect the eyes. Covering the nose and mouth with the mask, so you breathe through a layer of wool, has advantages in severe cold and wind. It is a little sloppy when the wool gets soaked with moisture from the breath, but the exhaled air warms the wool, which in turn warms the next breath. The mask is especially useful for sleeping. If the sleeping bag isn't quite warm enough, breathing cold air may be enough to cause you to spend a cold night.

It is important to discover how much clothing you need, and the temperature patterns in the area you are in. By experimenting you can soon arrive at a combination which is adaptable to changing weather conditions without carrying too many pounds or spending too much money.

Some people need a sweater or light down quilted jacket over the wool shirt. Others prefer a turtle neck, long sleeve jersey to a T-shirt. There is always a dispute concerning union suit versus drawers, which category now must include women's knit body suit underwear. (My wife offers a caution to the ladies: when buying the "body stocking" make sure it comes equipped with a backside opening; apparently not all do.) Overgarments such as wind and warmup pants are more versatile than long underwear and can be removed if the day is warm.

Avoid tightly fitting pants. Stretch ski pants are comfortable and sturdy, but close-fitting garments have a serious drawback—they cause more heat loss than loose ones. Tight clothing which lies against the skin will be warmed by the body; if snow touches the tight pants, it will melt, thus absorbing more body heat and moistening the cloth. Loose clothing, which holds a layer of air between skin and garment, may have some unmelted snow on it all day.

The boot-top-to-pant-leg gap is easily closed by a tie down strap or drawstring at the cuff, or by gaiters or leggings. Lace-up leggings have the same drawback as stretch pants, holding the fabric so close to the skin that body heat warms it. Waterproof gaiters cause a sweat condensation problem as serious as snow melting on the pants. Loose nonwaterproof gaiters with heavy durable zippers are the best choice.

Long gaiters are necessary with knickers, as the long knicker socks, being of wool with a long nap, don't protect the lower leg from wind and become covered with snow which melts. Knickers are comfortable, with little bind over the knee when you need to step very high, as is common in deep snow.

People who wear stretch pants or knickers often must wear long underwear because these stylish garments tend to permit greater heat loss than full length, heavy duty, loose wool pants. If you have to wear an extra layer of underwear to make up for a cold garment, it may be better to wear a single warmer one. Everything you do out in the snow is more complicated than on dry ground. A good illustration is managing suspenders: they have some advantages in that they hold the pants up without constricting the belly, but when you have a sweater, down jacket and windbreaker over them and are trying to find a sheltered spot to take care of nature's call, better be prepared to shiver as you fuss with your clothing.

Every item of clothing should have some degree of water repellency. Powder snow has a way of blowing and getting on and into everything, and snow falls off trees as you pass near. Conditions change in a matter of feet. The day may be too warm to keep water repellent wind gear on, yet the trees may be dripping. You may be swishing along in shirt sleeves on easy going, and round a clump of trees to discover a scramble up a steep pitch through snow-covered evergreens. So you go ahead and get all snowy because it is too much bother to stop and dig out the parka and put it on.

Keeping the feet warm isn't entirely up to the boots. If you have adequate or better clothing on torso, legs and arms, keeping all of them warm, probably mediocre cold weather footgear will be sufficient. But G.I. arctic Korea boots and down mitts aren't going to keep feet and hands warm if you are standing around in wet cotton pants and soaked shirt and jacket. If your blood is warm as it flows through arms and legs, it will do a lot toward keeping feet and hands warm.

Two pairs of socks will provide both cushion and warmth. If wool is irritating to the skin, wear cotton next to the foot. For an overnight stay be sure to dry wet socks, and carry extras. Wet clothing can be dried over a stove in a tent. Quite a bit of the warmth of leather boots is contributed by socks, so keep them as dry as possible. Lightweight leather boots are not adequate for cold weather, but if your boots are not warm enough don't try to solve the problem with more socks. It is possible to freeze one's feet by putting on more socks for warmth if the extra socks make the boots too tight, restricting the blood circulation. Expedition overboots or canvas mukluks are an effective way of making a single boot warmer. They will keep the boot dry and, as they extend up the leg almost to the knee, they add lots of protection with little extra weight.

The white G.I. Korea boot of rubber is probably the warmest footgear, but it is not readily available. Most commercial insulated rubber boots are very soft and really not very warm. All suffer from the common drawback that they are waterproof and hold sweat in the boot. This doesn't harm the insulation as it is enclosed between the two waterproof layers of the boot, but for some people it is unbearably wet and uncomfortable.

When using rubber footgear in which the feet are constantly wet, wear two pairs of socks for cushion and foot protection. The moisture softens the feet so they blister much more easily. After a long day in wet socks the feet begin to suffer an ailment called "dishpan feet," and after a couple of days' hard snowshoeing the bottom of the foot becomes tender and feels like one big blister.

Heavy mountaineering boots and commercial insulated boots of leather are probably about equal in warmth. In temperatures of around 15°F they are borderline. When standing around the feet will likely begin to get cold. Snowshoe bindings must be adjusted fairly tight for good control, which restricts blood circulation in the feet and causes them to chill more quickly. Expedition overboots add insulation to this fairly warm type of boot and may be enough for comfort in 0°F weather.

Shoe pacs and snowmobile boots which are constructed of rubber lowers and leather or fabric uppers don't provide sufficient support for the foot. When the bindings are tightened the pressure is on the foot rather than on the boot. Some people wouldn't use anything but shoe pacs, but in my experience, it takes a lot of socks, or a felt inner boot, to make them warm enough, and the binding will frequently bruise or blister the spots of greatest pressure (for blister treatment, see Chapter 10).

The warmest boot currently available is probably the double mountaineering type used by the American Mt. Everest Expedition. The inner boot is light leather with foam rubber or felt lining, enclosed in a very heavy leather outer boot. Designed for mountaineering, the boot has a heavy lug sole and hard toe, and bindings do not bruise the foot, even when cinched down. The boot is warm, but expensive and heavy, and like other leather ones, will get wet and must be kept from freezing if you camp overnight and expect to get it back on in the morning.

Improvisation is fine but can be carried to extremes. Avoid equipment or gimmicks cobbled onto something you already have that doesn't work right. These inventions give the appearance of increasing the adaptability of gear to many situations, but many are too complicated to be practical or require constant adjusting. Try to pick out clothing that you adjust only when it becomes extremely cold, extremely windy, or extremely warm. Time spent fussing with gear would be better saved for enjoying the scenery.

Chapter 5

OTHER EQUIPMENT

Tents

For general use in winter where high winds are no problem there are a variety of tent designs which make a choice appear difficult. However, it is of greatest importance to get the simplest pole assembly and the most room for the least weight. Snow travel is strenuous and you will be carrying enough gear without adding unnecessary ounces to the load.

Many outdoor retailers sell "expedition model" tents adequate for the most rugged winter outing on high peaks in the Cascades, Rockies, and Sierras, where heavy snow and high winds are the equal of summer storms in the Himalaya and Alaska. Not all "expedition" labels indicate better quality, however, so compare before buying. Real expedition quality tents will have much reinforcing on seams and corners and may be of heavier fabric, and so will weigh and cost more. The heavier fabric also may be more windproof and water repellent. Still, the lightweight tent can be protected by shoveling or shaking the load off during a heavy snowfall, and if you know the area and use the terrain to advantage, you won't need to lug a Himalayan quality tent. Do remember, however, that sheltered places accumulate more snowfall than wind-blasted ridges and plateaus, so be prepared to dig out more often.

Most tents lose a great deal of space in a simple A-frame or pyramidal design as the roof and sidewalls sag in unless the guy ropes are adjusted frequently. For example, a tent with a floor 5 feet wide and 7 feet long is hardly adequate for two people when the tent walls—or roof—sag in. However, 1-foot-high sidewalls will add enough room so that the two can put all their gear in the tent overnight, or bring in one more person, without gear. A-frame sidewalls which slope from ground level to ridgetop usually have guy ropes to help hold them out, but by morning they always seem to have stretched so that the frost-covered inside rubs on you when you get in and out of the sleeping bag.

The large pyramidal type suffers equally. The center pole is probably the greatest nuisance, although it is handy to tie a flashlight to for illumination since before-sunrise breakfast and after-dark dinner is the usual order of things in winter. A low silhouette, modified pyramid design with about 1-foot sidewalls is available. The weight per man is small and usable room much more generous than the tall, sagging, traditional McKinley and Logan designs.

External frames, which are about the only new modification in tent design in the last 20 years, add more useable internal space. The advantage of more room offsets the debit of extra weight in poles. The frame makes it possible to hold the roof out so the lower third is like an 18-inch vertical sidewall. This also eliminates the center pole and several outside guy ropes. All the sections of external frames are joined together by the small end of one slipping into the large end of the next. Vital sections may get lost as the tent is collapsed and rolled up in the morning. The solution to this problem is to run a length of elastic shock cord through the hollow centers of each section, then attach it on the inside of each end section, so that no piece can be misplaced. If there is some tension on the shock cord it is easy to join the sections together, especially when setting the tent up in a storm or after dark. For the tents with solid fiberglass pole sections, about all you can do is count carefully each time you take the tent down to be sure you have them all.

The average modern tent is made of nylon rather than cotton. Nylon can be lightweight and nearly windproof, quite water repellent and very strong. Coated fabrics have their problems: some are supposed to "breathe" but don't; most coatings peel. A rainfly is very useful in near-melting or rainy winter weather. Essentially a tarp shaped to tie over the tent, this second layer of fabric sheds moisture very well. If the weather is cold and dry, the fly adds warmth. It also can be used as an extra ground cover inside the tent or to cover gear left outside. It is desirable to stow all packs inside the tent to keep them from being buried in snow, although a small tarp can be used to cover these items outside.

Care must be used to protect the waterproof floor from cuts and scrapes which let moisture in. Foam pads provide floor insulation and are an absolute must instead of air mattresses, boughs, etc.

Ventilation is necessary, especially when cooking. Burning gasoline, kerosene or propane releases not only poisonous fumes but a large amount of water vapor, which may condense on the tent ceiling. Boiling water adds to this. It is frustrating to be wet in a good tent, which doesn't leak from the outside, because cooking vapors and the occupants' moist breath create enough moisture to condense on the walls and drop on sleeping bags, occupants, et al.

Sleeping Bags

Choice of a sleeping bag for winter will depend mainly on how much warmth one needs. This probably will have to be determined by experience either at home or on summer camping trips. For some people a bag with 2 pounds of down or polyester batting is sufficient, while others require double that plus an insulated jacket.

The insulating value of the down or polyester is dependent on the amount of trapped air. Down is extremely lightweight, and when contained as in a sleeping bag, has great insulating ability per pound of weight. Improved polyester filled sleeping bags deserve consideration. Their weight is greater than down bags for equal warmth, but cost is less. The main advantage of this synthetic fiber over down is in retaining insulating value when wet. This is of less concern in a sleeping bag, which is usually carried in a waterproof stuff bag, than in an insulated parka, which is worn in falling snow and under dripping trees.

Sleeping bag manufacturers have written at great length on the relative warmth of different types of construction. All agree that when the two layers of cloth which contain the down are sewn through or quilted, the insulating value is reduced. Next best is the system of inner and outer fabric separated by walls which in effect create separate tubes or boxes. These allow the down to fluff or loft, with no sewn-through part where the down is compressed. The warmest method of containing the down is that in which the individual separating walls of the tubes overlap. This construction prevents all but a few cold spots. There are minor variations within these three categories of construction.

Simplicity, warmth and roominess are of greatest importance in the sleeping bag. Frequently you are chilled when first getting in the bag and so have only removed down jacket and wind parka. Down-clad bodies are crowded on each side and after a couple of hours you awaken, uncomfortably warm. If the bag is roomy enough, either pants or shirt, or both, may be removed without unzipping the bag. These garments may be put on again inside the bag without the discomfort of exposing a lightly clad body to the cold air next morning.

The penalty for warmth and comfort is usually weight and expense. It is pleasant to emerge fully dressed and warm from the eiderdown cocoon, hands warm and efficient for starting the stove. The Spartan can survive in a tight, lightweight bag, especially for only one night, but winter nights are about twice as long as summer nights. It is not unusual to crawl into bed at 8 P.M. or earlier and remain there until it is light outside the next morning at 7 A.M. or later. If you are uncomfortable, these are long, dismal hours to suffer through.

Most bags have a zipper opening with a hood. The hood is of course vital in cold weather and should have a simple drawstring to cinch it down when the zipper is entirely shut, leaving an opening only large enough to breathe through. It is a mistake to breathe inside the bag, since breath is laden with moisture which will cut the insulating value of the down. The

Rest stop near timberline in Cascades near Snoqualmie Pass. Deep snow settles on a slope such as this, and pushes against small trees, causing them to lean downhill. They spring up after the snow melts.

snorkel, a 6-inch length of wool sock held in place by elastic and used as a breathing tube, is a real help in sleeping; the exhaled air warms the wool, and the inhaled air is thus warmed somewhat. Breathing cold air severely chills the body.

Some excellent sleeping bags have added gimmicks which cut the warmth considerably. Long zippers tend to be cold, even when special tubes of down lap over them. Some are designed to be zipped onto another bag to create a double bag for two, but generally these combinations sacrifice warmth and add weight and cost. Others have special drawstrings on the hood, including one around the neck. The last thing I need in the sleeping bag is a tight cord around my neck. Sometimes in winter the tent or snow cave seems confining. Falling snow packs against tent walls, further constricting already tight quarters. Great piles of snow falling out of trees hit the surface with dull thuds which make sound sleep in a snow shelter difficult. Snowshoers have been known to have nightmares under such circumstances, and rip their way out of the sleeping bag with appropriate grunts and snarls. The noose around the neck might be a handicap at such a time.

Packs

You will need something big enough to carry the clothing and extras necessary for a winter outing. An aluminum-frame pack with a large sack is better than a small rucksack jammed so full it is hard to find things. It takes more equipment to hike in the winter than in summer, whether on a one-day hike or overnight. If it is all inside the bag, it won't get as snowy as it will tied on the outside of an undersized pack.

The purpose of the frame in large backpacks is to provide a rigid platform to attach the straps and pack to. Its design holds the frame away from the wearer's body by wide straps. A rucksack has little, if any, frame, and usually is much smaller than a frame pack, limiting cargo space. Length is shorter, so no supporting hip strap is possible; if a waist strap is attached it is mainly used to keep the pack from flopping around on a bouncing, plunge-stepping, rapid descent. Although some rucksacks are large enough to carry full overnight gear, frame packs distribute the load more evenly among the shoulders, hips, and hip strap, and for carrying heavy loads are more comfortable and less fatiguing than rucksacks.

There is a wide variety of such packs with a wide range of prices. The more expensive ones are usually lighter in weight, with the bag made of nylon fabric. Frequently a manufacturer puts on a sales program promoting an improved design that is more or less of a gimmick. These changes include new suspension systems, zippers which give access to the bottom of the bag, or a series of separate compartments, each with its own opening.

The most valuable qualities are durability (so the pack will not fall apart and require time for repairs), plenty of room inside the main bag (so there will be no need to tie things on the outside), padded shoulder and hip straps (to support weight comfortably), several outside pockets (for goggles, compass, snacks, canteen, moleskin, and other frequently used items), waterproof fabric (so the gear inside will not get wet in a storm), and a large top flap (to completely cover the top opening and keep rain and snow from working in).

Frame packs can be adjusted to fit almost any size person comfortably. The shoulder straps should be shortened or lengthened to carry the load without being so tight that the frame bruises the back, or so loose that the back strap hangs down on the buttocks. The wide web strap across the lower part of the frame should rest on or just below the belt or waistband of the pants, usually a little below rather than above.

When this is accomplished, hunch the shoulders slightly to raise the pack, and tighten the hip strap attached to the bottom of the frame. This strap should buckle below the pants belt and above the crotch on the lower abdomen, about where low slung pants ride. All is in proper adjustment when the weight of the pack is carried partly on the shoulder straps and partly on the hip strap, thereby taking the strain off the shoulder muscles. Proper fit makes breathing easier: a heavy load on the shoulders impedes breathing and cuts down on the air supply to the lungs and blood, which in turn slows down the flow of nourishment to the blood and increases fatigue.

Section Two

TECHNIQUE

North Fork Teanaway River Valley.

Chapter 6

PHYSICAL CONDITIONING

Most people enjoy an activity until they become tired, but the more strenuous the activity, the sooner fatigue detracts from enjoyment. Actually few people enjoy snowshoeing for itself. Almost everyone who snowshoes loves the winter outdoors, which offers them an aesthetic, emotional, or even sensual enjoyment. They enjoy the beauty, the sense of being humble in the presence of magnificient mountains, the clean, crisp atmosphere of unspoiled wilderness, and the exultation of reaching a difficult objective. Snowshoes are merely the means of getting out into the natural scene rather than passively viewing it from a distance.

Physical fatigue not only spoils the fun of an outing, but exhaustion or near exhaustion may create danger by clouding perception and judgement. Tired parties may choose an apparently less strenuous return route only to find that fatigue-influenced shortcuts or alternatives become extremely dangerous or impossible routes.

Realistically, good physical condition is the best safeguard against emergencies. By conditioning you recognize your limits. You are more likely to avoid fatigue-caused errors because your mind is clearer. You will know when it is time to turn back because you have tested yourself and know if you can make it back. And if you can't, you can start building a shelter so that tomorrow, after some rest, you can start out early.

Because it is so inconsistent, traveling on snow is tiring. Snow conditions are usually determined by the temperature at the moment, complicated by elevation and the length of time since the snow fell.

Fig. 17. Walking with spraddled stance while carrying extra weight places distinctive strain on hip tendons.

At times 1/2 mile per hour is a fast pace on a gentle trail; other times may see a 3-mile-per-hour velocity for several hours. Under any conditions, however, snow travel is likely to be fatiguing compared to summer trail hiking.

Not only is footing poor, there are two extra burdens the body carries when snowshoeing: the weight carried on the feet and that carried on the back. As mentioned, the British Everest formula suggests the weight of snowshoes on the feet may be as tiring as carrying a 40-pound pack. The extra clothing and gear necessary to be comfortable in winter will often amount to 25 pounds for a day hike; in summer this would be adequate for overnight.

Snowshoeing puts an extra strain on the tendon in front of the hip joint which lifts the leg. Due to the spraddled stance required to compensate for the width of the snowshoes, this tendon receives unusual strain. The wider the snowshoe, the greater the strain. Compounding the problem is the high leg lift necessary to snowshoe through deep, soft snow.

Fig. 18. Extremely high "uphill leg" lift when traversing steep, deep snow.

When traversing sidehills, the uphill leg must be lifted higher than the downhill one, as the uphill snowshoe cuts more deeply into the snow in breaking out a trail. When traversing, and snow conditions are such that you walk in two trails, one slightly lower than the other, the uphill leg tires faster as it cannot be straightened out and relaxed with each step, but remains bent most of the time.

It is obvious that as one snowshoes the feet must point in the same direction as the snowshoes, especially with good bindings. When hiking on a summer trail it is possible to rest the feet and ankles by changing the direction they point. When hiking cross country some people go to great lengths to vary their foot position, climbing steep slopes pigeontoed or splay footed, or side stepping, first right side, then left side toward the hill. Most of these techniques are impractical on snowshoes, and the lower leg and ankles reflect the strain.

One last ache deserves mention. Rising on the balls of the feet when going uphill tires the calf muscles. However, letting the heel sag down flat on the snowshoe webbing stretches this muscle. Either technique results in some leg fatigue.

Anyone who climbs or hikes each weekend won't find it as necessary to condition. Most people, however, do not have that much free time. And late October, November and early December weather is often wet and cloudy, which curtails hiking and climbing but doesn't provide enough snow for snowshoeing. It is this late autumn and early winter period of forced absence from the hills that makes it necessary for almost everyone to condition muscles, heart, and lungs so that preliminary outings can be made with a minimum of misery.

It seems that the most effective dry ground conditioning for snowshoeing is attained by wearing the heaviest boots available while carrying, for an adult, 25 to 50 pounds in the pack. The leg muscles must carry the added weight of the heavy footgear in addition to the tonnage on the back. Bending over to balance the load, straining each step, comes close to duplicating the stance of the snowshoer struggling through deep snow.

Any type of conditioning—jogging, calisthenics, or whatever—is miserably tiring for the weak, or miserably boring for the strong. But suffering through a conditioning program will make the mountain hikes fun. Be miserable on the conditioning hill so you can enjoy the entire winter. After you have worked hard and forced your body to be strong, it will respond to your desires on a snowshoe outing, even when the going is difficult.

There is some sort of rise available for conditioning within a short drive in most areas. As a last resort, there are stairs, preferably outside. Many areas have favorite local hills used for conditioning hikes, some with organized speed events. But while this speed training is great for heart, lungs, and legs, it is not too similar to an 8 - 10 hour snowshoe trip. Speed in itself has poor carryover from dry trail to snowshoeing, largely because in aiming for greater speed, sprinters carry less load; T - shirt, shorts and tennis shoes are their usual garb. By contrast, a heavy load will force the slow pace and swaying movement typical of snowshoe travelers. Heavy boots or ankle weights are about as close as one can come to duplicating the effect of snowshoes.

Climbing hills with a heavy load in the pack and on the feet conditions the body to the type of strain that snowshoeing puts on it. The lungs must absorb oxygen into the blood stream and the heart pumps this energy-producing material to replenish the muscles, while the shoulders are burdened down and the rib cage constricted by the load.

Good conditioning for snowshoeing is a relative thing. The dedicated mountaineer and backpacker no doubt tries for a much higher level than the office worker who has no extensive background of trail hiking experience. Some people will never desire more than a level snowshoe hike of a few miles. Thus the program will vary to suit the individual's ambitions.

Offered as follows is a program for snowshoeing fitness for those who would like to climb major peaks in winter; it can be scaled down proportionately for lesser objectives. Twice a week, take a conditioning hike (in the evening if necessary). Allow 50 to 75 minutes for a 1500-foot elevation gain. Use heavy boots and, depending on your body weight, up to 50 pounds in the pack (possibly rocks). Descend without load. Repeat until this can be accomplished without special rest afterward. Every second or third trip take no load as a "bonus." After two or three weeks, cut down to one hike a week. Add a short mountain hike or climb every other weekend, building toward more strenuous hikes in six weeks or two months. If smoking or alcohol or drugs interfere with this program, eliminate them, as they will shorten life and good physical condition will lengthen it.

The purpose of this program is to build good hiking and climbing condition and maintain it year round. It is much less painful to recondition after a short layoff than after a 20 - year period of inactivity. Don't try to do it all at once like an over-eager youngster. If you are 40 and haven't done anything very athletic since your teens, be patient. If it took you 20 years to attain the degree of physical weakness typical of age 40, it will take a while to reverse the process. If you suspect some heart trouble or any serious physical weakness, have a complete physical examination before starting the program. Each hunting season finds a few weekend warriors whose enthusiasm exceeds the strength of the flesh to the extent that they expire. So begin slowly. The carcass you reclaim may, with care, be able to carry you far enough back into the hills to give you a new vision of the loveliness of winter hills and the worthwhileness of making the effort to get out and see them.

The psychological aspect of this program is vital: it must be regarded as a life or death matter. Without some physical strength your outdoor activities will cease. Your outdoor experiences will recede farther and farther into the past, and other activities will be substituted which will relegate the hills, mountains and backcountry and even snow-covered meadows beside the road to the days of "I used to."

This will take some dedication. But if you can get the vision of yourself, walking through areas where all evidence of man has been erased by deep snow, enjoying the clean, crisp, sparkling air, there is hope. There is a life to live which is richer and fuller if you can get away from the urban scene. In winter each of us can be a little stronger, a little better, than we usually are.

Chapter 7

WALKING ON SNOWSHOES

Snowshoeing is basically walking, the same movements as hiking, but with two important differences: first, the surface is inconsistant—stable and solid, or hard and slippery, or soft and bottomless—and all movements must reflect the condition of the snow. When traction is poor, or position precarious, move very gently, with the flowing, fluid movement of a cat stalking a mouse. Don't lunge or leap from step to step, especially on a steep climb or traverse or when making a kick turn, or thrust forward so hard that your snowshoe slips backward. Even on a crust continue to move more gently than you would on dry ground. Deep traction devices are a great aid, but often there is an icy spot in the midst of acres of firm snow, and this may cause an unexpected slip. Even the deepest traction does not grip on 4 to 5 inches of rather firm, dry snow on a crust, as in a wind slab, where the soft snow on top may be too deep for the traction to cut through to the crust below, yet the top snow will slide on the underlying crust.

The second difference in walking on snow is that the snowshoes are longer, wider, heavier, and more unwieldly than hiking boots. It takes some time to condition leg muscles to the wider stance. When walking slowly you center your weight alternately over the right and then the left foot. To thus balance on one foot you must move your upper body first a couple of inches left, then a couple of inches right as each step is taken. Snowshoes emphasize this action. The extra weight on the feet tends to cause the snowshoer to take a longer, slower stride than normal, part of the adjustment to walking on snowshoes without undue fatigue.

Another reason for using a longer stride when snowshoeing uphill is that in loose snow it is necessary to step far enough that the new step is not undermined by the previous one, especially if the steps sink 8 inches or so into the snow. Short, choppy steps have more of a tendency to cause a lunge and unnecessary slip. The effect on a traverse is that the tail of the forward snowshoe will slide into the previous step, and any slip results in some sliding downhill. Usually this is of no consequence, but if the route goes through a narrow slot between two trees, even a slight misstep can dump the unwary into the tree hole below.

Generally the ax is used as a walking stick on level going. On hillsides it should be in the hand on the uphill side; the ax is usually too short to use on the downhill side for balance. Sometimes it is best to lean on the ax just a little on a sidehill to make sure you don't accidentally overbalance, but it is easy to quickly shift it to the downhill side if necessary to prevent slipping. Ski poles require a little more planning to use efficiently. Longer than an ax, they require more time to place accurately. For level going, never bring the baskets ahead of the feet; actually push on the poles like a cross-country skier, which will help propel you along. Carrying a generous portion of your weight on the poles eases the strain on the legs, and a good high leg lift, necessary for breaking trail in deep, soft snow, is easier to achieve.

The greatest energy-saver, and a vital aid to pacing yourself, is the rest step, a momentary pause between steps. With a little practice you can adjust the length of the pause to the state of your fatigue. As you step forward, thrust the front snowshoe out and let it plop down, or stamp it firmly in place. Straighten the rear knee joint so the tendons and cartilage are holding your weight; pause, and relax the thigh muscles, using the poles or ax to maintain balance. Bringing the rear leg ahead, thrust the snowshoe out, place it, lock what is now the rear leg, relax momentarily and repeat. The effect is to rest the legs during the actual time they are working hard. A couple of seconds of work, a couple of seconds of rest, makes it possible to keep going steadily without long stops during which extra clothing must be dug out of the pack to prevent chilling. The rest step is a real help when climbing and breaking trail in deep, loose snow, which requires a high leg lift, with special strain on the tendons in the hip area. The brief rest between steps does more good than infrequent, long, sitting-down rests.

The pause during the rest step works to advantage in loose snow for another reason. The snowshoe is moved forward and stamped down, then after a pause you move gently forward and put your weight on it as the other snowshoe is moved forward and stamped into the snow. By stamping the snowshoe down two things are accomplished. First, the snow is packed somewhat: even powder snow will firm up—the beginning of age hardening—if there is a pause between placing and putting weight on the snowshoe. If it is done in one motion, without pause, you will sink deeper because it will pack at a deeper depth as your full body weight comes down. Second, the snowshoe cuts into the snow and grips it, not only with the traction device, but also with the crosspieces and webbing. Try to pack the steps at turns and other crucial points.

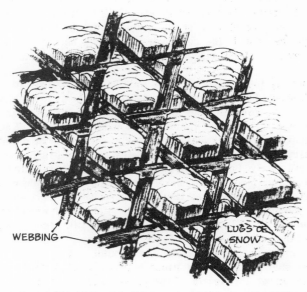

WEBBING —

LUGS OF SNOW

Fig. 19. Snowshoe webbing bites into the snow, forming lugs and providing traction.

Take turns breaking trail. In loose snow the trail-breaker may have several extra pounds of snow on his snowshoes. This isn't balled or stuck on, it just falls on top of the webs when he sinks perhaps 8 to 10 inches.

Sometimes it is possible to break trail for 5 minutes continuously when climbing steeply in loose deep snow; other times it may have to be reduced to as little as 2 minutes before changing leaders. An advantage of this system is to make it possible for each person in turn to really force the pace for a few minutes while he is breaking trail. If there are five people taking turns, each will get 12 minutes rest between 3 minute turns in the lead. As his time for breaking trail ends, the leader steps out of the way and drops to the rear as the rest of the party moves on past.

Usually ascend at a grade a little less than the maximum angle the snowshoes will climb (the maximum angle of course requires that you hang on with great effort on the verge of slipping, and is very tiring). Use an angle of ascent which is comfortable and lets you relax somewhat. At the point of turning, for example to the right, plant the left snowshoe firmly and stamp it in so it will hold. If you are using an ice ax, place it in the slope above the binding of the left snowshoe and work it in securely. Ski poles should be planted below the snowshoes, alongside the boot heels. Then shift weight to the left snowshoe and ax or poles, face the slope and swing the right snowshoe around to point in the direction the next switchback will take, and shove it into the snow.

Make sure you place it so the tail is not on the left snowshoe. Stamp the right web into the snow, and gently shift weight and step on it.

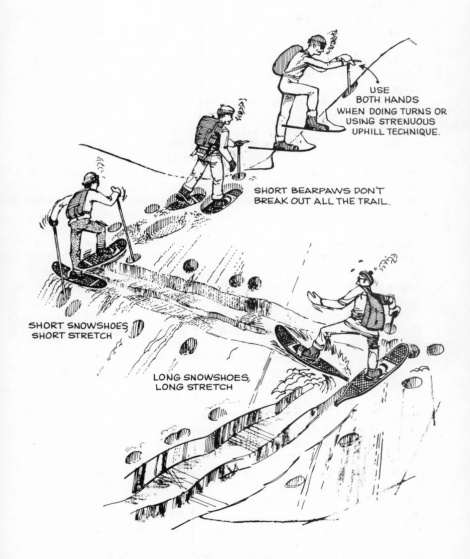

Fig. 20. Making switchback turns, and, at top, toeing straight in on steep pitch.

Try to stay well above your previous trail, which has undermined the snow you now are building the turn on. Reverse the procedure for a left turn.

The very short, narrow aluminum frame snowshoes allow a modified technique. The 8 x 25-inch model, for example, requires merely that you kick steps as for snow climbing without snowshoes. These webs are so small that they do not interfere seriously with placing your feet on turns.

As each succeeding snowshoer uses the turn the trail shoulders slough off and late comers may have a harder time getting around than the leader. By all means use special care in placing snowshoes precisely where they were placed before, widening and deepening the tracks for those who follow. Special care in placing snowshoes, ax or poles, will pay dividends in avoiding slips. Sometimes there is only one way past an obstacle. Be sure to preserve the trail so others following do not have to rebuild it.

There are other ways to make the snowshoe turn easier. Plan to use the gentlest places on a slope for the turns; look ahead and pick the route to use the terrain to your advantage. Avoid the steepest parts and don't hesitate to make short switchbacks between turns. Use trees and their branches for handholds. When the snow is soft enough, the trail can be two snowshoe widths wide and relatively level, but usually the snow is too firm for that and requires one snowshoe trail slightly above the other. People on 36-inch and shorter snowshoes have an advantage in this situation as these short showshoes may be placed one ahead of the other. This keeps the feet at the same height, which is less tiring than the two-trail technnque. Beavertrails overlap some and can be used almost single file, but still are at a disadvantage compared to the 8-inch width on sidehills.

Balance is critical when placing one snowshoe ahead of the other. Ordinarily the feet are spaced widely enough apart for good stability. But traversing with the snowshoes single file decreases stability, so the poles or ax must compensate. A person with short snowshoes may save some effort on a traverse, but at the expense of irritating someone in the group with the long Yukons.

Another benefit of using short snowshoes with forward mounted bindings is their practicality for kicking the toes in and climbing straight up a steep pitch. As this technique is strenuous and requires soft snow, it is limited to short pitches. Long slopes with enough soft snow to kick the toes in for a good step could be steep and unstable enough to ava-lanche (see Chapter 11). The method is to swing the snowshoe backward and flip the tail up. The toe is kicked straight into the slope, with the web horizontal and the tails sticking out in the air. The forward-hinged 36-inchers and shorter shoes work well for this; a strong snowshoer can use 10 x 46-inchers, too, although it is more difficult. Obviously the snow must be right—soft enough to kick the snowshoe in about 12 to 16 inches and still firm enough to support the snowshoer.

Long steps, spaced wider apart laterally, are necessary, as the

Fig. 21. Traversing. **Left**, single file traverse with short snowshoes. **Right**, traversing usually develops two trails, one above the other.

lower step, deep as it needs to be, badly undermines the step above. Steps such as these are weak and do not form a trail adequate for a large party. The main use of this technique is along ridges where drifting creates slopes too steep to angle up, and without enough room to switch-back around the obstruction. With more skill and practice you will find other places where a short steep pitch climbed straight up may save time. Although admittedly of limited use, this technique is one more way to save energy over a long pull.

Techniques such as the kick turn and toeing in straight up are easier if you can extend your legs and take long steps, placing the forward snowshoe in undisturbed snow which has not been undermined by other steps. Movements must be smooth and precise, which may be a little too much for the untrained muscles of beginners, who experience "sewing machine leg" when fatigue begins to build up and overextended muscles begin to protest. Muscle spasms cause a jerking that probably precedes a real cramp.

As you travel more on snow it will become apparent that patience is necessary to enjoy winter travel. Snow is too difficult a surface to travel through to expect to race in, see the view, and sprint out. During the winter months there are fewer daylight hours at a time when it takes longer to get anywhere. Take time to enjoy the trip—make the scenery along the way as much a goal as the destination. Patience also means not getting upset by minor equipment problems and changes of plan. A broken strap or loose rivet is never convenient to repair, but should be fixed before it becomes major breakage. Be sure to get camp set up in time to get adequate rest. Realize that snow is inconsistent and revise your schedule if necessary. Take time to avoid possible avalanche areas. Do a good job of routefinding, trail breaking, and camping, and if necessary give up an objective if the danger from storm or avalanche is too great. The penalty for error in the winter is much greater than it is in the summer.

Chapter 8

MOUNTAIN SNOWSHOEING

Mountain snowshoeing is like lowland snowshoeing, only more so. The terrain varies from level stream valleys to steep mountainsides, and even the more gentle trails often have a section of switchbacks or a sidehill to be dealt with. The snowshoe must meet the entire range of slopes from gentle to steep, and all types of snow, often on a one-day hike.

Snow is at all times sensitive to an infinite variety of modifying conditions. The only predictable thing about it is that it will be different higher up, around the corner, or over the ridge. Temperature is the determining factor in the condition of the snow. Cold temperatures are associated with powder snow. A crusted condition is due to changing temperatures: warming and thawing melt the surface, then cold temperatures freeze it. The areas which have warmed the most will refreeze, pack, and become the most firm. Generally the temperature is colder at higher elevations, dropping approximately 3°F with each additional thousand feet.

The textbook set of snow conditions would be slush in the valley bottoms, with powder snow on the upper slopes, and variations of both between. Conditions seldom follow the pattern exactly because forest, cloud cover, wind, and direction of slopes create microclimates.

For example, a fresh snowfall may remain powdery until storm clouds pass and the sun comes out. Then sheltered open south slopes may become slushy from valley floor to ridgetop on a warm afternoon, freezing at night into an iron-hard crust. A thick stand of tall evergreens just above the valley bottom may shelter powder snow for several days after the storm has passed and temperatures have warmed, yet snow melting off the trees may refreeze under each tree into an icy patch surrounded by powder. North slopes may not warm up for weeks at a time, and so have deep powder most of the winter. Ridgetops cooled by constant wind do not develop crust, yet may be wind-packed hard as ice. Nearby may be a patch of powder cooled by the wind, yet on the side facing the sun, or slush on the lee side of a clump of trees, sheltered from the wind and warmed by the sun.

The force of gravity is another factor modifying the behavior of snow on slopes of mountains or hills. A fresh, stable deposit of snow, when sufficiently warmed by the sun, may begin to flow like water and avalanche into the valley bottom. Or the wind may blow certain areas free of snow, depositing it in extra deep layers in sheltered locations.

The most immediately noticeable effect snow has upon the mountains is to subdue harsh lines of foothills and create Alaskan giants out of modest Cascade, Sierra, and Rocky Mountain summits. Ugliness is hidden and rugged heights are accented for the viewer who leaves the road and travels over the snow.

To meet the great variety of conditions found in the mountains, you need to know which snowshoe works best on varied terrain (see Chapter 1). Don't be tempted to get a Yukon on the theory that deep snow is the only problem in the mountains. First of all, the snowshoe must be used on sidehills, making narrow width of prime importance. When more than 2 feet of snow falls, the trail ledge on sidehills begins to disappear. Even sections of road drift over in exposed places. Gentle trails beside streams become snowed over and develop formidable slopes which descend steeply into the water in midwinter. If an otherwise simple route crosses the creek and there are 4 feet or more of snow on the ground, it will be a struggle to get down one side and up the other unless you have a shovel and snowshoes designed and equipped to climb well. Trees on sidehills have deep wells — holes in the snow around the trunks — which must be detoured around, perhaps on steep slopes. Fallen trees and drifts on gentle sidehills can create short, steep slopes on otherwise easy hikes. And the mountaineer on the ridgetops is often following a narrow path beside cornices and over drifts.

An 8-inch-wide snowshoe can be edged if the snow is not too hard, but not nearly as effectively as a climbing boot or ski. Wider snowshoes of course are just that much less effective. Bindings are too flexible to really "hammer" even narrow snowshoes into hard snow on a sidehill. The nearly straight frames on some models hold better than the curving sides of the bearpaw and beavertail.

The variety of slopes and snow conditions in hill or mountain country tends to present situations that are harder on snowshoes than open country. The main cause of a broken frame is stepping on a hole or de-

Ridge top is icy, although powder snow conditions had prevailed to this point.

pression in such a way that the toe and tail of the shoe are on higher points than the middle of the foot, with perhaps the middle 24 inches of the frame bridging the hole. Often ridgetops are blown free of snow, revealing sharp rocks and frozen clods which cut webbing and damage frames. There are many obstructions lightly covered by snow, such as trees, branches and rocks. A gentle step may do no more than scratch the frame, but jumping off something may create enough force to break the frame or cut the webbing. (Snowshoers seem to delight in jumping off things as the soft landing is so different from crashing down on bare ground.) But stepping into small depressions, jumping onto hard, hummocky snow, wading rocky streambeds, and falling into tree holes are the most common damaging maneuvers.

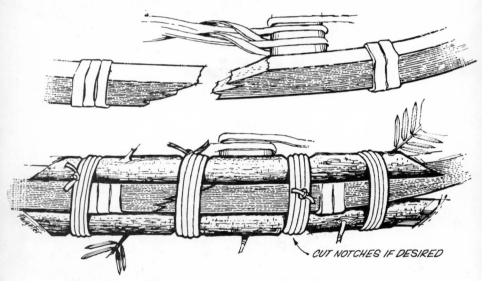

CUT NOTCHES IF DESIRED

Fig. 22. Repairing a broken frame. **Above**, broken frame. **Below**, splint of branches on broken frame. Four wraps of cord will hold in place.

First aid for a broken frame is the same as for a broken bone. In forested country, cut a couple of small branches to use as splints, lay one on top and one under the break, and wrap tighly with cord. This will last quite well, especially since the snowshoer will then be much more careful how he steps down on his footgear. (For repairs to broken webbing, see Chapter 1.)

By all means get good equipment. Any advantage is worth a few dollars more when conditions become difficult and you are tired. A small equipment failure or a minor injury may cause only an unpleasant night out in summer, but in winter may result in frostbite, or may actually be fatal.

Chapter 9

ROUTEFINDING

A glistening snow cover mantling the winter landscape is a thing of magic, giving mountain and hill country such an allure that more and more people each year are drawn to explore its beauty. However, reaching a chosen goal presents a different problem than the summer hiker is accustomed to solving.

Even distant backcountry can be reached by trails in summer, since the main problem in trail routefinding is choosing the proper fork at junctions. Storm and bad weather have relatively little effect on this type of routefinding, and maps and trail guides are usually adequate reference material.

Deep snow changes all this by covering not only the trail, but also trail signs, blazes on trees, and even trailside shelters. In heavy timber there is frequently a lane through the trees, but in more open country all trail signs disappear. In places exposed to wind and drifting snow such obvious features as roads disappear altogether. Ridgetops are changed the most — drifts 20 or 30 feet high alter the visual aspect of the landscape and knolls appear where gullies were in the summer. Some of these changes are for the better, as a great deal of brush and garbage is buried, and some gullies are filled with snow, making easy creek crossings where wading was required in summer, or leveling out a depression.

The snowshoer's problem in winter is more similar to that of the summer backcountry traveler who goes beyond the trails: a route is chosen through obstacles such as cliffs, stream gorges and impassible thickets, but rather than routefinding by trail junctions, he is looking for topographical features such as the places where two streams or canyons meet. Instead of counting mileposts he is relying on other landmarks.

Although it is desirable to be able to see where you are going, especially in new country, it is best to be so familiar with the area that you are able to recognize small landmarks if the weather is cloudy and major landmarks are hidden. The key to this is preparation. Choose winter objectives you have been to in summer, or make certain there is someone in the group who knows the area. Not all trail sign is hidden, but it takes an observant person to discern a blaze on a tree down in a hole where sheltering branches have created a depression in the snow around the trunk, or a limb which has obviously been chopped or sawed off, or a section of Forest Service phone line almost hidden in the snow. Study the summer trails and note their location in regard to features which will show clearly in winter, so that if you lose a trail you can continue and pick it up farther along.

One danger in mountain country that must be checked visually on the spot is potential avalanche slopes or chutes. The new 15 minute (1 inch equals approximately 1 mile) U.S. Geological Survey quads showing forest cover give a hint as to possible locations of avalanches by contour lines indicating a steep slope in an area without forest cover. U.S. Forest Service maps are of no help in this, nor do summer hiking and climbing guides generally provide this information, although some summer trails cross or ascend slopes which frequently avalanche in winter. Observe the route carefully for avalanche chutes, recognizable as gullies swept clear of trees and leading unobstructed to ridgetop snowfields. Stay out of these potential funnels for the snow above, and do not hesitate to change the route from an open gully to a forested slope.

The easy part of routefinding is getting to the objective — a viewpoint, mountain top or a snow-covered meadow beside a stream. Like summer hikers, snowshoers are inclined to relax when following the return trail, and indeed usually it is as obvious as a summer trail. But in windswept areas take extra precautions, for a change in weather can create conditions which make returning extremely difficult unless the route is marked by brightly colored plastic flagging tied on trees, or by bamboo wands (garden stakes 2 or 3 feet long with flagging attached) which may be carried along and placed in open treeless areas. Flags and wands should be picked up on return and carried out. It may be hard to be serious about marking what in clear weather is an obvious route, but clouds and storms can eliminate even a prominent set of tracks and obscure the landscape so that each clump of trees, each ridge or draw looks exactly like every other one. On a clear day the snowshoe trail appears as a slash across each open spot, but a few minutes of blowing snow can totally obliterate it. In suddenly cloudy conditions even flagging and wands are not too effective unless they are very close together or you have taken and recorded compass bearings for the return trail.

The simplest method of taking a compass bearing back down the trail is as follows: face in the direction you will be traveling, and with the

It may be less tiring to remove snowshoes and kick steps up a firm, steep slope than to attempt to ascend it on snowshoes.

compass a safe distance from any magnetic object such as exposure meter, watch, ice ax, etc., let the needle stop swinging. (A good place is on your mittens laid on the snow.) Set north on the compass on the north end of the needle. Sight across the compass from the point where you are toward the direction you will want to return. Record this figure.

This is all that an amateur needs to know to get across an unmarked area when visibility is poor. Greater expertise is required if there are long distances to travel by compass and changes in direction are necessary at places where there are no identifying features, but the procedure is the same. On the return set the compass out, let the needle stop swinging and set north on the dial to the north end of the needle. Walk in the direction your notes indicate, trying to keep on the proper heading, and you should arrive at the next known point without difficulty.

This knowledge is a real safeguard in high, open country above timberline. Frequently the snow is so firm no real snowshoe tracks are left. If clouds move in, and a little snow blows into what tracks there are, there occurs a condition known as a white-out, when clouds merge with snow and all visual landmarks are hidden. The effect can be so complete it is hard to tell where the surface is until your snowshoe actually touches it. A white-out can be very confusing even on a small open area, but if you can travel from known point to known point by compass you are well prepared for the task.

The most difficult routefinding is in featureless, rolling country such as the foothills on the fringes of the mountain rainges. Most mountain areas are simpler in that the valleys are so deep and the features so prominent that you cannot get out of one canyon and into another without realizing you have crossed a divide. In gentle country you can be on or near a divide and cross into another drainage without realizing it, and follow it down away from the starting point.

The compass is of little help unless you are at a known point and want to get to another known point. To find your way cross country without a trail, you must prepare the information such as compass bearings on the way in to have the accurate information necessary to get out in a storm.

Snowshoers are getting farther into the mountains each winter. In addition to the increased avalanche danger from heavy snowfall in steep country, a new challenge is being accepted in winter glacier travel. Routefinding is the same on a glacier, winter or summer. Note the crevasses, which remain open all winter, and pick a route around them as you would in summer. The hollows are usually safer as the glacier surface is under compression and crevasses seldom occur there. Areas where the surface is shoved up, as a large mound a quarter mile or so across, generally are crevassed heavily, since the surface is under tension.

In winter there is much less indication of crevasses than in summer, when there is no snowfall and warm temperatures cause faster glacier movement. Unless the distance and depth are very great, wind-blown snow may bridge even wide crevasses by the same process which builds snow cornices out 10 to 20 feet on the lee side of ridges. When the "cornice" does bridge the crevasse, the snow drifts on across and leaves no clue that a few feet down there is unsupported snow. It is doubtful that any but small crevasses fill completely with wind-blown snow and there are many holes under the apparently innocent, smooth glacier in winter and summer. One additional problem in winter is that it is difficult to locate crevasses by probing with the ice ax. The snow is so soft everywhere that plunging the shaft in to the head does not necessarily indicate a crevasse underneath.

Snowshoes decrease the chance of stepping through a weak snow bridge by distributing the weight over a large area. It is likely that only a very wide, weak bridge would collapse under a person wearing footgear 3 feet long. However, in winter as in summer, keep the party roped up.

Crevasse rescue on snowshoes is the same as with crampons, except that the boot heel, rather than the toe, is placed in the slings, unless one can remove snowshoes while hanging from the climbing rope without losing them down the crevasse. Raising techniques are described in **Mountaineering: The Freedom of the Hills.** As in summer, ice axes must be used for belays (the ice ax basket must be removed for this, so be sure it is quickly detachable).

In summary, several things for beginning snowshoers to remember are: first, be familiar with the area you are in. Second, follow a trail if possible. Third, when the trail is obscured by snow pick a route which avoids dangers and obstructions and is guided by prominent landmarks. Fourth, mark the return trail with flagging or wands in case it storms and landmarks are not visible for the return; carry a map and compass and correlate them with your route. Fifth, have an alternate plan for survival if you must stay overnight or longer and wait out a storm.

These rules are not fun and games — there simply isn't enough dumb luck to supply all who need it.

Chapter 10

ILLNESS AND INJURY

Hypothermia

With the exception of avalanches and extreme cold, the hazards of winter mountain travel are much the same as those of summer. However, any small problem such as a minor injury is intensified by winter conditions; cold is the catalyst that can create real trouble from difficulties which might be joked about in summer.

In a typical situation, a party is caught by a storm in a mountain area. The first reaction is to continue. Someone becomes tired, so others help him, and they keep going. Soon it becomes apparent that they cannot make it out, so they decide to stay overnight. By this time everyone is too wet and tired to set up good shelter, and because they never intended to camp in a storm, they did not bring the necessary equipment to do so. This can and does happen in summer, but is obviously more serious in winter.

The combination of fatigue, wet clothing and cold weather puts too great a strain on an individual with a physical weakness. An undiagnosed minor heart problem, or infection, in this situation can be fatal. Some people who have become severly chilled may simply die while others equally miserable survive.

In actual cases in which these conditions have occurred, and in which there have been fatalities, the party has tried to take care of its own problems, the first step in any emergency. But safety is due more to advance preparation than to individual or group heroics during an emergency. If the groups that experienced the fatalities had carried adequate overnight gear the outcome might have been very different.

Hypothermia is a more precise name for what is still often referred to as exposure. The problem is that the victim is unable to maintain normal body temperature. When inner body temperature drops below 96.8°F, shivering begins and coordination becomes poor. If chilling continues until body temperature is about 88°F, shivering stops and the victim becomes disoriented and enters a stupor. Unless something is done to stop the loss of body heat and restore normal body temperature, the victim will loose consciousness and die. The air temperature may not be below freezing and the victim may have no frostbite or frozen fingertips or toes.

Diagnosis is simple: the person is thoroughly chilled, somewhat disoriented, and his coordination is poor. If he can be warmed he will soon be back to normal, but if hypothermia occurs when a party is lost in a snowstorm and has no tent or tarps, the problem is very real. If a tent is available, set it up, strip off the victim's wet clothing and place him in a sleeping bag with another person in good condition for body-to-body warmth, or fill canteens with warm—not hot—water and put them in the bag with him. Hot drinks may suffice if his condition is not serious.

The timing of treatment for hypothermia should be preventive. Warm the chilled person before he becomes disoriented or enters the advance stages. The serious hypothermia case develops when there is no easy way to provide shelter. Adequate shelter, hard work and some real adapting to miserable weather are necessary to warm a badly chilled person in a winter storm or to bring a person already in hypothermia at nightfall through the night alive. Tents, sleeping bags and foam pads provide the best shelter and insulation, but even these must be properly used, and only expedition quality tents can survive winter storms above tree line; otherwise camp must be made in some sheltered place.

Nylon tarps may provide some protection in a sheltered area, but insulation is required underneath for sitting on the snow. Plastic tarps won't survive in a wind, but can be a ground cloth, or several people can wrap up in one and huddle together for warmth.

Snow caves are excellent protection, but it takes about 2 hours to dig a minimal cave for two with a shovel, and even then you must have insulation. With a stove in the party, and thus heat to dry the gear and prepare hot fluid to warm chilled bodies, a snow cave becomes quite liveable.

A snow trench or shelter built among living uncut boughs under a tree are other alternatives, both requiring shovel and tarps to provide any degree of protection in winter. Wind and snow blow through the boughs, but they may help break the wind if you can wrap up in a tarp. A trench will quickly drift full unless there is a good tarp for a roof.

An igloo is excellent shelter but requires more skill to construct than a snow cave. It is also time-consuming and requires a snow saw, perhaps a shovel, and again a foam pad. (For more on snow shelters, see Chapter 12.)

Other means of warming a person are in the Mountain Rescue category. Probably the most effective is a hydraulic vest, a series of flexible plastic tubes attached to fabric that covers the torso of the victim. Water is heated in a pot on a stove and a simple hand pump used to circulate the heated water through the tubing spaced out on the victim. Propane tent heaters may be used to provide heat for the victim. However these are not regular gear taken on snowshoe hikes. All the possible emergency gear you might need would create a prohibitive load.

It seems that certain individuals lose the will to live when in a difficult situation. The fact that one of three survived in two different recent situations would tend to indicate some emotional collapse in the ones who succumbed. Good physical condition is an invaluable deterrant to the "psyching out" which can affect you if you are tired, cold, and lost. Choose companions who are in good condition and choose objectives within your capabilities. Take short hikes before trying a long, arduous one, to screen out persons who fatigue easily and to work yourself into excellent shape. If you are with a bunch of "tigers" it may be possible to persevere through the worst of conditions; if anything goes wrong you are much better off than with a soft group whose members are new at the activity.

Plan what to do if you are running late, get lost or "confused." Assume leadership and force a stop to set up camp before the party is exhausted, wet, and about to collapse. Avoid leading a weak group on a tough trip. It's fine to be the strongest in the party until it becomes a life or death matter, but a close call from an avalanche or storm, or a fatality due to your own poor judgement is not easy to live with in the years ahead. Most of all learn when to turn back.

Check the weather. Storm clouds are dismal everywhere. In fact, it's worse in a storm on the inspiring peaks than in the foothill forests. For the high ones, wait for good weather; you will make miles with less effort and have a view beyond description.

If the temperature is zero degrees or colder, be especially careful not to overextend yourself or the group. Be ready to return to the car if someone is too tired, or his feet or fingers become too cold.

Frostbite

During extremely cold weather a person may freeze the tip of the nose, cheek, ear, finger or toe during an outing, but unless an entire foot or hand is frozen, this is not too serious. Flesh is damaged first by freezing, and then may die of oxygen starvation as blood circulation is cut off. Frostbite is painless. The nerves usually signal for some time that the part is cold, but freezing apparently prevents pain by numbing the nerves, and the only sensation is that the body part is very cold. All snowshoers have cold hands and/or feet some of the time, so it is necessary to check visually for frozen areas.

Treatment is to restore circulation by thawing the part. Mild surface frostbite often can be thawed by contact with warm flesh. The tissue eventually turns brown or blisters as from a burn. Blisters will heal readily unless they are broken and scraped, or rubbed, or become infected. Heavy drainage from blisters on a frozen foot or hand that has been thawed will soak up a lot of dressings. Try to keep the area clean; makeshift dressings can be sterilized by scorching over a flame.

Freezing a hand or foot solidly is more serious. Treatment is the same but more difficult due to the extent of the injury. Thawing is done very gently without any rubbing or abrasion. Contrary to the time-honored fallacy, do not rub by hand or with snow as this will tear the blistered flesh and increase damage.

A sheltered place such as a tent, snow cave or igloo is desireable as working space. Heat water over a stove to about 105°F, and put the frozen hand or foot in it. Once it is thawed, protect the part from further mechanical damage, especially from re-freezing. Bandage and protect it carefully and elevate it to promote circulation.

Before thawing a badly frozen foot the whole situation must be evaluated. Once thawed, the victim should not walk out, as tissue damage may be very serious; he must be evacuated on a sled or in a helicopter. However, if this is absolutely impossible, and the choice is to either walk out or sit for perhaps days in a very poor spot, he had better walk out before the foot is thawed. Of course the longer the part is frozen, the greater will be tissue damage due to oxygen starvation, but this may be the lesser of two evils. The decision will have to be made on the spot.

Sunburn and Windburn

A day, or even a few hours, of sunshine is so delightful in winter that snowshoers may tend to forget its devastating effects on exposed human flesh, particularly when compounded with reflection from snow. Be sure to carry adequate sun cream, or cover with clothing as necessary.

Equally painful is windburn, which must be prevented by proper clothing.

Wind Chill and Overheating

Wind chill factor plays a prominant part in both hypothermia and frostbite. Wind gives the effect of a colder temperature than the thermometer shows. For example, 15°F with a 20 mph wind is equivalent to a temperature of -17°F with no wind. Mountains and ridges do queer things with wind currents. In a sheltered place you may be warm and comfortable while 100 feet away a steady wind is blowing. Clothing should be adaptable to quickly meet changing conditions.

Avoid exposing the bare hands for any length of time at low temperatures. Use a snowshoe binding that does not require removal of mitts. Learn to strap on crampons and close zippers wearing mitts (a length of cord tied on the zipper pull makes a hold large enough to grab with mitts or gloves). Learn to snap photos with mitts on; many Himalayan climbers have frosted their fingers when taking pictures on summits, and in their befuddled state of mind did not notice until too late that their fingers would not bend.

Observe if your hands are easily chilled and take special care of them if this is the case. Warm them under armpits—your own or a companion's—before they become dangerously cold. (Some people condition their hands to adapt to the cold by intentionally leaving mitts off as much as possible when working outdoors between winter outings.) Be prepared to cover your face if necessary; wind on the bare face can be painful even if it is not causing frostbite. Don't gasp for breath and risk frostbite in the lungs.

With a little careful checking you can discover at home whether you are protected from wind. Start at the bottom. The first gap is between boots and pants. You should have tie-down cuffs or gaiters, and wind pants. Next is the pants-to-shirt gap; a short shirt tail won't stay in when you are carrying a pack or bending over. The underwear or undershirt should cover the gap if the wool shirt doesn't. The wind parka and the insulated jacket should extend down to mid-thigh.

The abdomen and stomach should be protected well, as this is the heat generating center. Next the neck and face: can wind and down parka hoods be cinched up tightly to leave only nose and goggled eyes out? If not, better make some adjustment. The second layer of protection is the cap-face mask, which you should be able to tuck under the lower edge of the goggles. It should cover nose, mouth and extend down the neck to the shirt collar.

For winter the goggles should have side protection. A cold wind blowing ice particles under ordinary sun glasses and across the eyeballs will have much the same effect as snow blindness (sunburn on the surface of the eyes). Check the wrists: can parka sleeves be pulled down to cover the wrist of the wool mitts and sealed with elastic cuffs? This is desirable, as it is sometimes hard to keep overmitt gauntlets high enough on the forearm to protect the wrist, where the large artery carries warming blood to the hand.

In contrast to wind chill is overheating on sheltered slopes. Cooling is desirable to limit the sweating which dampens clothing and cuts its insulating value. When you are down to wool pants and shirt, there isn't much more you can remove, although occasionally a T-shirt is enough in a sheltered area, even at 0°F.

Roll shirt sleeves up, unbutton the shirt and put mitts and cap in the pack. This opens up neck, head and wrists, where there are lots

Cathedral Rock from Mt. Daniel. Note slab avalanche fracture on righthand side of Cathedral.

of arteries, as well as the chest and belly, to cool air. Some people use fishnet T-shirt and drawers, and unbuttoning the wool shirt or pants with this string garment underneath does promote cooling. Pants cuffs can be rolled up unless you will kick too much snow on your socks.

March Fracture

Besides cold-induced injuries there are mechanical risks to the sport of snowshoeing. The wet, sticky snow that packs in a ball on the snowshoe webbing under the boot can be more than just a nuisance that must be removed to avoid an awkward downward angle of the feet in descending. When the snow builds up under the arch of the boot there is danger of fracturing a small bone in the foot. (This is fairly common among marching soldiers and so is called a "march fracture.") The best prevention for march fracture is a stiff soled climbing boot.

Blisters

Snowshoe bindings cause a lot of blisters, especially when the boot is soft and flexible and does not take the pressure of the binding. Since the weight, when picking up the snowshoe to take a step, is on the top of the toes, this is an area that blisters often. Heels suffer on steep sidehills, or when climbing steep slopes. Since snowshoes cannot be edged effectively, one must walk as on crampons, with the snowshoe flat on the sloping surface and with a bend in the ankle. This is not only tiring, but puts a lot of pressure on the side and back of the heel, and the heel bones.

Take lots of adhesive tape, moleskin or adhesive foam and a few bandaids. Cover tender areas with moleskin or tape before they blister. As soon as a tender place develops, stop and perform first aid. If you use moleskin be sure to take a small scissors or a knife to cut it to fit. After sticking it on, add some strips of adhesive tape to help hold it in place. Once in a while the edge works loose and forms a lump which makes another blister. If the blister has formed, drain it carefully with a sterile needle and apply moleskin and tape, or apply protection to relieve the pressure and leave the blister to dry up. Be careful when you remove the adhesive material at home so it doesn't pull off a large piece of live skin attached beyond the blister. Apply disinfectant if the blister has been abused in this manner.

If the blister is due to a rough spot on the inside of a heavy leather boot, carefully carve the lump with a wood chisel until it is smooth. Smooth all the wrinkles in your socks as you put your boots on, especially when you wear two or more pairs. Check for lumps in the socks, which may be wads of lint.

The problems discussed in this chapter are, except in unusual circumstances, preventable. Proper equipment, good judgement, and careful attention to early warning signs should make their occurrence as unlikely as some rare tropical disease, but there is always a crop of neophytes, or an old-timer who has not learned his lessons well. In contrast, the hazards described in the next chapter cannot be controlled by man, but must be recognized and avoided.

Chapter 11

SAFETY

Many of the objective hazards of winter travel cannot be predicted with any great degree of accuracy but must be observed and evaluated at the given moment. It is possible to say a particular slope is prone to avalanche, or that large globs of snow fall off trees after heavy storms; on-the-spot judgements must be made in each particular case as to the immediate danger.

Lakes and Streams

Snow travelers in the Canadian north, Alaska, and parts of the snow belt in the midwest and northeast occasionally fall through the ice covering a stream or lake. This hazard is less in the Pacific northwest and the mountain west where high lakes are generally frozen and snowed over deeply enough to be safe to cross. Springs with a relatively warm temperature are then the main hazard: the warmer water tends to melt the ice where the spring enters the lake, causing a weak spot. Generally mountain streams flow too fast to freeze into good access routes.

The main problem caused by streams is that they are open and deep all winter. Eight to 10 feet of snow on either bank makes them as formidable as a crevasse in a glacier. If there isn't a bridge or a footlog, the hike may necessarily end at the stream crossing. Even when there is a bridge, it may not be safe to cross. Walking on a narrow ridge of snow 8 feet above the bridge decking and a longer way above the streambed calls for flawless technique: side-step across very gently, keeping the feet directly over the log or bridge. This may leave snowshoe tails and toes hanging out in the air if the log is narrow. It may be safer to clear the snow off the log before walking it, although this may expose frozen and icy bark. Traction devices 1 to 1 1/2 inches deep give considerable security on slippery footlogs and icy stones in streams, biting into these surfaces much better than any rubber soled boot. If the water is deep, unhook one shoulder strap and the waistband of the pack to make it easier to jettison in case of a fall in the water. If a rope is available, it is a good idea to rope up, or rig a hand line for safety on dangerous stream crossings. It may not be possible to catch someone before he lands in the creek, but it will insure his getting out.

When there is no log or bridge, or where one is impassible, it may be possible to shovel or dig a trail down the snow wall on one side of the stream, step across and climb up the wall on the other side. Be careful to keep your snowshoes out of the water if traveling in powder snow, for several pounds of powder will freeze on wet snowshoes in the first steps, unless they happen to be plastic.

"Idiot makers"

Part of the attraction of winter is walking among snow-covered trees—they can be even more lovely than in summer. At times they are covered so deeply that no green shows, and the top or a high branch may have an accumulation weighing many pounds. Periodically these huge bombs, called "idiot makers," fall out of trees 100 or more feet tall, landing with a "whoomp" and making an impact crater in the snow. I know of no one who has been injured by one, but from personal experience, I know they can knock you flat. Keep a wary eye open when the trees are carrying heavy loads of snow in their tops; wearing a hard hat isn't too bad an idea in this situation.

White-outs

White-outs have already been mentioned as they affect routefinding. In conditions of dense fog, cloud, and often blowing snow there may be no visual clues to location. Sky and snow merge and the horizon disappears and it is difficult to tell whether you are walking uphill or downhill. Until you touch it with an ax, pole, or snowshow, it is impossible to tell where the surface is. Frequently people walk off drifts and tumble because they simply cannot see the dropoff. Several spectacular falls of nearly a hundred feet have occurred on Mt. Rainier from the ridge beside the Muir snowfields onto the slopes above the Paradise Glacier. Fortunately no injuries resulted, but all the victims' companions knew was that somehow they had disappeared. The only way to move in a white-out is very carefully.

Head of Early Winters Creek from summit of Liberty Bell Peak. Avalanche chutes run from ridgetops to valley floor, sweeping trees from their paths. Dense stands of trees have probably never been swept by slides. Areas dotted with trees, between the dense stands and obvious avalanche deposition sections, may experience a major slide every 50 to 100 years. In the intervening years, trees sprout and grow until the area is again devastated by an immense avalanche. A loop of the North Cross State highway is visible at lower left.

Avalanches

By far the most spectacular hazard in winter is the snow avalanche. Large avalanche chutes descending through heavy forest from ridgetop snowfields are easy to recognize and avoid. Small slides are a greater hazard than huge ones because there are more of them and they aren't as obviously powerful and destructive. Man is totally outmatched when caught in sliding snow: a layer only 6 inches deep and 20 feet wide sliding less than 100 feet can bury a person. Big avalanches involve tremendous tonnages of snow and develop a great deal of momentum. Besides ripping out trees on the edge of their paths and in the areas where they stop, they run up opposite slopes. Some travel long distances on level ground after a rapid descent. When speed is high the mass climbs up hillsides where the containing gully makes sharp turns. When the snow drops over a cliff in a gully there is a roar like thunder. Nature on the rampage, as these avalanches testify, is an awesome thing.

There are three main conditions causing snow to slide off mountains. First, during a storm it builds up to a depth and weight that exceeds its ability to adhere to the snow or rock surface beneath, so it slides, frequently during the storm itself. Second, wind picks up snow on the windward side of ridges and deposits it on the lee side, or in any sheltered place. This layer may slide during or soon after the storm as a loose, unconsolidated mass. Or it may settle into a firm mass, and over the course of days or weeks the bond between it and the surface below may weaken until the entire layer slides as a slab. The third condition is a rising temperature that melts the newly fallen snow. The mass is lubricated by this moisture, and the bond with the underlying snow is decreased until either the upper layer or the whole mass slides.

When a layer of snow is unstable, anything which disturbs it can trigger the slide — a snowshoer, skier, snow falling out of a tree or from a cliff above. Avalanche control methods in ski areas and on highways include explosives to trigger the snow into sliding, or to stabilize it further when it will not slide.

Avalanches follow gullies off the sides of ridges and down mountain faces. These may be spotted easily where there is forest cover. Lee slopes below cornices are common areas of wind slab. Snow cornices indicate lots of wind-blown snow on the side they overhang. Forest cover isn't foolproof, as snow can slide through fairly closely spaced trees like water, inflicting additional injuries as the victim ricochets off trees. Only if the trees are "as thick as the hair on a dog's back," to quote one U.S. Forest Service ranger, can you be sure it will not slide. In one actual instance, a slide filtered a skier through very closely set trees, stripping him of skis, poles, hat, glasses, and mitts, and inflicting severe injuries.

The Colorado Rockies and Utah's Wasatch Mountains are famous for powder snow avalanches, which generally occur at high elevations where temperatures remain cold. Much powder snow sloughs off the steepest slopes during storms; it is most dangerous where wind has deposited piles of it in sheltered gullies. The speed of the sliding snow is great, and the air pushed ahead of the avalanche results in a preceding wind blast which is as destructive as the snow itself. The powder snow menace is not usually as severe on the volcanic peaks of the Cascades, possibly because they are quite rounded and have few high sheltering ridges where it can collect. On these open slopes the wind packs the snow as it falls, while behind the sharp, jagged ridges in the Rockies and Wasatch greater quantities can drift in. However there are places on Mt. Rainier where wind-blown snow accumulates and creates avalanche danger. Between 11,000 and 12,000 feet the Ingraham Glacier, in the lee of Gibraltar Rock, catches enough snow to plug, or at least cover, its many huge crevasses each winter. At another point just under 7000 feet, Panorama Point faces into the prevailing southwest wind. Here it forms both slab and powder avalanches which have killed at least one of the many people who snowshoe, ski and hike up it toward 10,000-foot Camp Muir each winter.

When a pile of windblown snow on a lee slope congeals into a somewhat solid mass, it is called a slab. As it settles, the slab adheres to itself and tends to shrink, and the process weakens the bond with the underlying layer. The joint between the two layers may develop depth hoar, which looks like frost crystals. This zone is less dense than either the slab above or the snow below, and the area sounds hollow underfoot. As the bond weakens, it eventually reaches a point at which the slightest jar can trigger a slide. When it slides, the slab, several inches to several feet in depth, breaks off from stable snow in a vertical fracture which may run for several hundred feet. The sliding mass may start over a large area and break into many blocks. The danger in a slab avalanche is that many tons of snow may remain poised for weeks and then be released all at once. Apparently not as sensitive to rising temperature as powder snow, many slabs are triggered in the Cascades in April and May by overhanging cornices crashing onto the snow below. Of course cornices themselves, which may form on both sides of a ridge within a short distance, are a hazard to anyone below, whether they trigger any further avalanche or not.

Slab is formed by conditions of heavy snowfall and high winds in mountains, hills, and even on flats. These slabs on flat areas also sound hollow and sometimes settle a little with a "whoomp." If the snow on the flats is settling as you snowshoe over it, there will be slab formations on the ridges too. Normally the deeper your web sinks, the firmer the snow becomes, but occasionally your snowshoe will settle through the snow, which seems to be hollow, or softer, underneath. This may be an indication that you should not venture out on steep, high mountain slopes for a few days until the snow has stabilized.

Wet snow avalanches are the most predictable type and are most typical of the wet, warm Pacific northwest. The textbook sequence of

Winter view south from Mt. Daniel, Cascade range. Steep slopes of Bears Breast (right center) and Overcoat, Chimney Rock and Lemah Mtn. (left to right on skyline) avalanche frequently in winter. Note fresh avalanche from face and in gully on Bears Breast, and cornice with drifted snow on lee slope in foreground.

events leading to release of these heavy, relatively slow-moving slides is as follows: cold moist air from the Pacific Ocean moves across the Cascades, dropping several feet of snow. This air mass is pushed out by a warmer one; the snow is warmed to melting, becomes wet and settles. Weight increases as it picks up water from the warm, moist air. The bond between the new snow and the underlying layer beneath becomes lubricated and the mass slides. Wet snow a few inches to several feet in depth can slide. Weight is very great although speed is slow when compared to powder snow. Wet snow rolls into balls, ranging from a few inches in size to blocks several feet across. It normally freezes to ice when it stops.

There is much discussion among snowshoers of what to do when caught in an avalanche. If you can still think and react to the situation it seems best to get on your back, trying to stay on top of the sliding snow with swimming motions of the legs and arms, attempting to work to one side. If you are standing and the snow you are on begins to slide, sit facing downhill. Actually no one seems to have very satisfactory evasive tactics or secrets of survival. My own experience in two avalanches was that it was over so quickly there wasn't time to do very much. Both times I turned and faced downhill. In a few seconds my feet worked through the sliding snow and caught in the layer underneath, then the sliding snow behind pitched me forward on hands and knees. This is not the way to ride an avalanche because my head could have hit any obstruction first and the powder eddying around my face made breathing difficult. Once at the mercy of the avalanche I no longer had any choice in matters of direction and position.

The best cure is prevention; minimize the time you are exposed to the danger. Cross narrow chutes one person at a time with lookouts posted to warn of an approaching slide. If the day is warm and there is deep new snow with no recent avalanches around, get to a protected place. Wet snow slides are more frequent on warm afternoons than crisp cold mornings. If there is no way around an avalanche hazard, the outing must be ended. Some persons who are exposed to avalanches use avalanche cord, dark colored nylon cord about 1/8 inch in diameter and up to 100 feet long. One end is tied to the waist and the rest is dragged when crossing a particularly dangerous area. Should a person be caught in a slide, there is a good chance of a part of the cord showing, clueing his rescuers where to dig.

In areas of man-managed avalanche control, such as Cave Ridge on Mt. Snoqualmie in the Cascades, a snowshoer can run an additional risk. Explosive artillery shells are fired at ridges above roads and human habitation to trigger small slides before the snow becomes deep enough to cause a really damaging avalanche. Be sure to check with local authorities before entering areas subject to such control.

There is no accurate way of predicting the hour, day, or week of most slides. The longer the exposure to danger the greater the likeli-

Dumb luck in action. Gully is hard and icy, but has avalanched recently. Snow has sloughed off below snowshoe trail, taking one snowshoer with it. Lookout (silhouetted at right) could do little but shout a warning if another avalanche should occur.

hood of getting caught. The best one can do is to recognize that deep, unconsolidated snow on steep open slopes is likely to slide soon after a storm. Warming weather after heavy snowfall will quickly cause avalanches. Lee slopes are very likely to avalanche after heavy snowfall accompanied by high winds, and the danger will remain for weeks after the storm. Obviously the only 100% sure way to avoid getting caught in an avalanche is not to be in a place where there might be one. There is seldom any totally safe time during winter and into early spring. The higher elevations do not firm up as soon as lower slopes. Cornices fall off ridgetops until June or later.

The conditions I prefer for a trip into an area of avalanche hazard are several days of warm, clear weather following a storm, then clear, cold, stable weather. The warm weather should flush off the avalanches and cold temperatures stabilize the snow.

Experienced judgement is the only way to assess the danger, and then it must be based on knowledge of recent weather and the terrain. The only choice you have, in the final analysis, is to accept the risk and enter an area of hazard, while minimizing it as much as possible by hurrying through one at a time, or crossing the danger zone early in the morning, or to find an alternate route with less hazard. Spending the remainder of one's life in the few seconds it takes an avalanche to run really doesn't seem to be a truly meaningful snowshoe experience.

Chapter 12
SNOW CAMPING

Shelter

More care and planning are needed for snow camping than for dry ground camping, which can be as simple as rolling the sleeping bag out under a tree, crawling into it and going to sleep.

It might seem that digging a snow cave or building an igloo rather than carrying a tent would save time and energy. But considerable skill and work are necessary to create a snow shelter equal to a lightweight, roomy, modern tent, and one cannot count on having snow in the quantity and consistency required. The snow cave and igloo really are not practical unless you intend to use them for more than one night, or have plenty of time and energy and just want to experiment. A half hour is enough time not only to set up a four-man tent but to get all four in it and supper started. Two hours of hard digging is a minimum for a four-man cave or igloo by persons with average skill; realistically, 3 hours will probably elapse before one can expect to move in. The self-sufficient party has a larger margin of safety. If conditions prevent reaching the camping area desired, or if you get to the right area but the shelter is buried and cannot be found, or you cannot dig your cave or construct an igloo, you still must have shelter. Tents have to be the first choice, especially in somewhat unfamiliar country.

Winter camping usually involves a group no smaller than four to six because it will take this many people to break trail for 6 to 8 miles in hill country when conditions are less than ideal. A large tent provides shelter at low per person weight. If three two-man tents are used, the weight of tent will be from 12 to 15 pounds total, over 2 pounds per man; if rain flys are added, the total weight is almost 3 pounds per man. An 8-pound, four-man tent, and a 4-pound, two-man tent will average 2 pounds per man. Four men can set up the larger tent about as fast as two men can set up their two-man tent. When conditions are serious, a tarp or tent can shelter double or triple the number of people it was designed to contain.

Knowledge of the area you are going to be in is really helpful. Some excellent camp spots may not have room for a large tent, but small tents can be fitted in quite well. Although tents have drawbacks, the 5- to 10-pound weight of a roomy tent for four isn't that hard to carry, and the ease and speed of setting it up tip the scales in favor of the tent rather than the snow cave or igloo, unless the snow shelters are necessary because the location of camp is so wind-swept that only the most rugged expedition model tent could survive. For the average snowshoer these tents are too heavy, expensive, and limited in usefulness (see Chapter 5 for more information on tents).

Anchoring the tent ropes in snow can be quite a problem. Snowshoes and skis make solid anchors, provided the tent is to be folded first thing in the morning before they are needed to travel on. At times the snow is so soft that snowshoes are needed to move anywhere outside the tent. Packing the tent platform may be a job too. After you carefully pack with snowshoes and level the place to pitch the tent, you remove the webs and sink in to the knee. Then the platform is packed again by foot. But if you step off the twice-packed spot, you sink in to the hip.

In forested areas it is easy to find a few pieces of dead branch for tent stakes. Without this aid, be sure to carry your own stakes, about 1/2 x 12-inch dowel, or wood split like kindling. Place these through the loops sewed on the tent, or on the ropes, press or stamp into the snow, and pack snow over them. These small "dead men" are very secure. At times rocks exposed by wind can be used for anchors, although usually such places are too windy for a comfortable camp; the wind popping the fabric interrupts sleep.

If the snow is blowing it is necessary to seal the door and put up with condensation. Completely waterproof fabrics in this situation prevent any moisture from passing through the fabric, and can cause near-rainfall conditions within the tent. Enough snow to wet the top of your bag can blow in through a zipper not completely closed.

Camping in wet weather in winter may seem foolish, but it may happen unplanned. The weather may be sunny when you start out, but before the day is over a storm moves in, yet you have to stay the night. Too, the storm may pass through and the next day will be fine. Sometimes it may be cloudy and wet in the valleys, but up high, above 10,000 feet, it is cold and clear. Then it is practical to put up with a day or two of storm to get to the higher scenic area where it's sunny and dry. There are times when some of the group are so ardent there is no way to talk them out of starting on the trip even in near-blizzard conditions. Only when they are sufficiently wet and miserable do they accept the fact that an outing in a winter storm truly can be worse than no outing at all.

Snow caves provide the maximum protection from storm but are time-consuming and tiring to construct. The usual problem is that the excavators get tired before there is really enough room to be comfortable. It's a bad day when you must dig your first cave and spend the night in it and it is 8:00 P.M. and dark before you start.

Obviously careful thought must be given the location for a snow cave so nothing will fall on it and snow won't drift over and seal you in. During a Mountain Rescue Winter Training Session near White Pass, in the southern Washington Cascades, some of its participants decided to dig their caves on the lee side of a ridge. The windward side was too hard packed, besides having a wind and drifting problem. This slope was not steep, it leveled out below and was out of the wind, and so a whole string of caves was started, side by side, to house 30 or more persons. Real progress was being made, as the snow was deep, soft enough to dig well, but not so soft that a cave roof would fall in. To the surprise of the entire group, the slope avalanched. The tunneling had cut loose a slab avalanche which carried the Mountain Rescue people a short distance down the slope. Among the many things to be considered in the location of the caves, avalanche hazard was the only thing overlooked in this otherwise ideal spot. If you have a choice between a flat sheltered by trees, or an open slope where the digging is easy, be sure to consider avalance hazard before deciding to spend the night on the slope.

Two items are handy for actual construction, a snow shovel and either a snow saw or a folding pruning saw. An excellent shovel can be made by cutting the blade of an aluminum grain scoop shovel off so it is 12 inches long; if longer it will hold too much snow. Small aluminum snow shovels are poor tools for digging a snow cave, but will suffice in the absence of the heavier grain scoop shovel mentioned. A folding orchard pruning saw is lightweight and in some instances can be used to cut through an ice layer that the shovel cannot dent.

Carry good rain gear and extra mitts and rubber gloves in anticipation of this wet job. One cave on Mt. Adams was built for four in a blizzard at temperatures of about 15°F to 20°F. We became quite wet while out of the wind working in the hole, but the moisture in our parkas froze as we traded positions and went back out in the wind; the ice made a windproof garment and discomfort was minimal.

Some locations are less satisfactory than others for snow caves, a flat place being the worst. First a hole must be excavated straight down. When the hole is deep enough — 6 feet or so — tunnel in horizontally for the room, while someone else tosses the snow up out of the original hole. A slope is useful because the snow dug out falls out of the way. Usually some of the last of it must be thrown out, because as the cave reaches a depth of 6 to 8 feet the shovel operator cannot throw the chunks out beyond the entrance.

Fig. 23. Shallow-snow-depth one-man cave. Stomp snow first, then excavate 1, 2, and 3. Join caves, leaving dividing arches intact. Fill entrances to 1 and 2, close entrance 3 with pack and plastic.

There is a real technique to digging that far into snow. Of course the snow depth must be a foot or more deeper than the cave is high—too shallow a roof, less than 12 to 18 inches, may collapse. The snow at the bottom and rear of the cave may have settled so that the shovel can be jabbed only a couple of inches into it. Then each chunk must be chipped loose on three sides and pried off the wall. Too much pressure can easily bend cheap, lightweight, aluminum shovels, which must have been designed to merely paw loose snow around. However, it is possible to study the mechanics of the problem and develop a technique to dislodge the most material with the least effort without breaking the shovel. A shortened grain scoop is quite strong and superb for this job. This is digging at its worst, reaching overhead as well as underfoot and working in awkward positions. Even more discouraging is encountering a stump or mound of dirt which forces excavation in a different direction.

It is much better to find a slope and tunnel straight in. Some diagrams show a very low opening with a high domed room beyond. The problem with this design is digging through the small opening on your knees or lying down. For speed make the door high enough to dig in a fairly comfortable stance. Snow caves need plenty of ventilation, which the high door provides. Take a small plastic or nylon tarp to hang in the doorway. This will be adequate to keep the weather out unless there is a real storm raging, in which case you may want to develop a deeper, more elaborate cave.

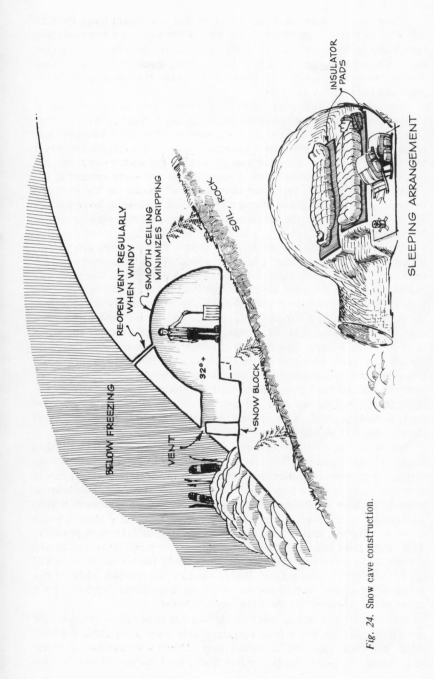

Fig. 24. Snow cave construction.

The cave is different from a tent in that you cannot bulge the wall out with an elbow or shoulder. If the wall is touched, snow trickles down onto sleeping bags or clothing. Foam pads are the best insulation on the floor. Some pads are so light in weight that you may be tempted to carry several to better cover the floor of the cave, which somehow always turns out to be lumpy and hard.

Once in a while it is possible to spend enough time with a good shovel to dig a cave with plenty of elbow, sleeping and cooking room. The first such luxurious cavern I observed had a very low entrance so all heat was trapped in the smoothly domed chamber, but the instructional diagram had showed no vent hole. As supper was cooked on the gas stove, the oxygen became exhausted to the extent that the one heavy smoker in the group nearly fainted. Realizing the cause, all bailed out and soon recovered. A hole was poked through the ceiling, releasing body warmth along with carbon dioxide, carbon monoxide and various cooking odors, and admitting oxygen.

A cave such as this is a luxury, since sounds such as wind, are stilled, giving a real sense of security to those within. Not all sounds are muted, however. Another cave I occupied had several drawbacks. The first was that we had not intended to dig it, but the February snow was so deep that we could not find the Forest Service shelter we had intended to use. So we dug a cave in a flat area, since there was no convenient slope. We also dug into a tree and left a branch sticking out from one wall, which dripped water on one sleeping bag all night. The trees outside were so loaded with snow from the storm that from time to time a branch would droop low and the immense snow load would slide off, landing with a loud whoomp! At intervals this muffled thud would awaken me to consider the difficulty of digging out of a collapsed snow cave. This would probably have been impossible with several feet of snow packed around me and the sleeping bag zipped up to my nose.

Igloos are equal in protection to snow caves but more than equal in the skill required to construct them. They are more subject to snow conditions; dry snow is almost impossible to work with. Under ideal conditions an expert can whip up a four-man structure in about a half hour by himself. As with a snow cave, any snow butcher, with a minimum of skill and enough persistence, can build an igloo. Generally allow 3 hours or so for the job, unless you have perfected your skill through practice. Two snow saws are more efficient—one for the man cutting blocks and the other to carefully tailor each block to fit the two surfaces it will touch. A shovel is also helpful; if only one saw is available, a shovel can be used for either cutting blocks or fitting them. Some people prefer a carpenter's saw to either the snow saw or shovel.

One expert igloo builder advises a homemade snow saw of the following specifications: use a piece of tempered aluminum alloy about 1/8-inch thick, 2 inches wide and 26 inches long. Attach a wooden handle to one end, leaving 20 inches for the cutting blade. Hacksaw serrations in it for

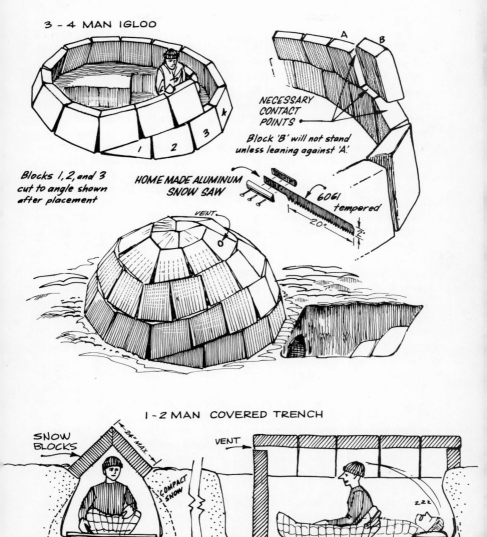

3 - 4 MAN IGLOO

A B

NECESSARY CONTACT POINTS •

Block 'B' will not stand unless leaning against 'A'.

Blocks 1, 2, and 3 cut to angle shown after placement

HOME MADE ALUMINUM SNOW SAW

6061 tempered

20"

2"

VENT

1-2 MAN COVERED TRENCH

SNOW BLOCKS

24" MAX.

VENT

COMPACT SNOW

zzz

END VIEW — *Expand for second person* — SIDE VIEW

Fig. 25. Snow shelter construction. **Above**, three- or four-man igloo. **Below**, one- or two-man covered trench.

the cutting teeth. This allows you to cut blocks up to 20 inches high, making it possible to dome over the igloo roof in about four tiers of blocks.

Cut the first tier at a slant so that the second tier will spiral up. Cut the door out after the wall is somewhat above it, since it is hard to cut out a block long enough to extend across the door opening and strong enough to support the wall above. Bevel the top of each tier inward to slope the walls inward toward the top of the dome. If the top of each tier is horizontal, you will end up with nearly vertical sidewalls and have trouble drawing them in to close the top. The person laying blocks must work within the circle as the tiers rise. Some prefer to cut blocks from the floor, excavating a foot or more of depth, which cuts down on the height of blocks to be laid. Ideal size for the blocks is about 12 x 18 x 6 inches. Uniformity is more dependent on the skill of the block cutter than the condition of the snow, but the more uniform the size and shape of the blocks, the easier it is to lay them in position. Don't try to build too high, as it is difficult to fit a block if you must raise it much above shoulder level. The keystone, or capstone block must leave an opening for ventilation; this is less of a problem than in a snow cave but still necessary.

As in snow caving, rubber gloves are useful; long gauntlets will keep snow from working into the cuffs of your sleeves as the last blocks are raised to position. All chinks must be caulked. With powder snow it may be desirable to melt water and splash some on any weak places. An entrance tunnel may be built, although most people are ready to quit before then. A plastic tarp may be rigged to cover the opening, especially if held in place by packs on the inside.

The inside surface must have no points from which moisture can drip. The greatest disadvantage of snow shelters becomes obvious when temperatures rise above freezing. The ceiling drips, especially at the top of the door and vent hole. The humid air may be saturated by vapor from boiling water and stove emissions. The interior of the igloo is illuminated by light filtering through; if light is visible through the ceiling of a snow cave, it is too thin and may fall in. The white walls of both cave and igloo reflect light so well that one flashlight or candle usually is adequate for lighting.

Other types of snow shelters include a dug trench roofed with snow-shoes or dead branches and a tarp and covered with snow. Long snow blocks may be tilted together to roof over the trench. It is a good idea to be familiar with several of these shelters. In some places and conditions where it is impossible to use one type, another will work.

The permanent log and stone shelters erected by Forest and Park Services are excellent in winter, providing protection which cannot be matched by tents or snow shelters. However tents should be carried on trips to the large volcanoes even though there may be a stone shelter at the intended destination. Many people become benighted on these feature-less slopes in storms, frequently without proper snow conditions or enough time to construct a snow shelter. Weather problems are so much more severe in these unprotected heights that it requires Himalayan-type equipment and physical conditioning to weather storms above the protection of valleys and forests.

No matter how fast you can put the tent up, dig the cave or build the igloo, allow plenty of time for the job. Tent ropes become tangled, or the weather and/or snow may be uncooperative. Winter days are short. At 47° north latitude the sun sets at 3:30 P.M. during the dark, dismal season of late December to mid-January. Heavy cloud cover further cuts the limited daylight available, and some deep valley bottoms have no direct sunlight from mid-November until early February.

Be aware of these damp, cold spots and prepare for them. Cold air settles to the valley bottoms in these shaded areas. Sometimes it is much warmer a hundred feet or so up the south-facing hillside above the cold holes. It may be worthwhile to make a short climb out of the valley bottom to camp in a warmer spot. The most ideal summer camping spot will be the place to avoid in the winter — summer campers want a cool spot and winter campers want a warmer one.

Moisture is the great problem in winter. Sleeping bags dampened by breath or body moisture become progressively colder at night unless they are dried out (this is only a problem on outings of several days; after one-night stands they can be dried out at home). On sunny days they may be hung on a tree to air.

In a roomy tent clothing can be dried over the stove. Wet mitts and socks are a chronic problem, especially on a trip of several days. Following a storm it may be desirable to start a wood fire for drying. But in many areas trees are scarce and scenic and should not be used unless it really is an emergency, and life, rather than comfort, depends upon a fire.

Fires

For emergencies and in lowland forest areas where dead trees abound a fire is a real luxury or a lifesaver. Starting a fire in winter is not always easy, and again preparation is the key. Practice on day hikes. Carry a piece of candle, a fire starter made of rolled newspaper soaked in canning paraffin wax, or pitch wood. Break off a good supply of small dead twigs from near the bottom of a tree trunk; these are usually kept dry by sheltering live branches above. Occasionally you may find a dead tree with an abundance of dry, dead branches, but this is rare. Ignite a pile of twigs with the fire starter, and add larger pieces of wood, being careful to keep the flame going. A fuzz stick, a dry piece of wood with shavings carved in it, is an alternative where dry twigs are unavailable. A fire-resistant platform must be provided to keep the fire from melting down into the snow. A piece of light sheet metal, hinged to fold small enough to fit in the pack, is ideal. It may be suspended above the snow by baling wire attached to trees or stakes driven into the snow. Cut green wood to build the fire on only in case of an emergency to actually save a life, as living trees are too valuable to cut and burn for a mere marshmallow roast. An old standby that is handy for blowing on the kindling to provide a draft is a length of plastic or rubber tubing. The draft gives the flame a boost and saves the face from soot and the lungs from inhaling smoke.

If you can get some flames started in an area about 6 inches across, the fire will probably go. By the time the flames are a square foot in extent with a good bed of coals, good size pieces of wood which are fairly wet may be added, and the heat will dry them and continue burning. Sometimes desperate methods must be used, such as carrying a pint of gasoline, a highway flare, or a half pound of old inner tube, to get the blaze going. Many outdoor manuals show solid tablets of fuel and other fire starters. But for real performance under difficult circumstances these are inadequate for the job at hand. Most sure-fire aids are as heavy as a stove. It is usually hard to get a fire going under winter conditions, even when fairly dry dead branches or squaw wood are available. At times it may be impossible because moisture in the air has saturated even dead wood. Some areas just do not have enough firewood for the number of people who camp there. Generally it is not practical or desirable to depend on using a wood fire.

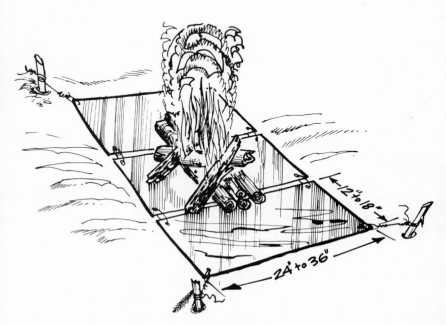

Fig. 26. Fire platform of light sheet metal suspended at preferred height by wire from stakes driven in snow. May be folded for easier carrying.

Stoves and Cooking

Although open fires are not practical in a snow cave or igloo, cooking over a stove in a tent or snow cave is not easy either. Extra care must be taken to clear a place large enough to set up the stove. Any spillage of fuel or food lands on the sleeping bags or the floor, making frequent house-cleaning necessary. For this reason it is a good idea to use a simple menu for meals when conditions such as storm or extreme cold or a pre-dawn start make it necessary to cook inside the shelter.

Lightweight stoves which burn three different fuels are on the market at present. White gas, butane or propane are the most popular for winter use. Kerosene requires more fussing to pre-heat the burner so the fuel will vaporize and burn cleanly. Extra gas or kerosene is more compact and weighs less than the equivalent compressed gas cartridges, which of course must be packed out. Start the stove before going on a trip, to make sure it works properly and to make sure you know how to operate it. Gasoline stoves are especially dangerous. All must be preheated so the burners vaporize the fuel before it squirts under pressure from the orifice. This is why you must burn enough fuel in the priming cup below the burner to adequately preheat the burner. If the valve is opened too soon, the gasoline is not vaporized and flaming liquid gasoline squirts out. Quick action is needed to close the valve, as it is easy to run the priming cup over, resulting in a small amount of flaming gas on the floor of the tent—and a possible flash tent fire that could turn a mountain outing into a disaster. The tent is the one abode that is susceptible to man's oldest enemy—uncontrolled fire. Practice lighting the stove in the wind, too, at home, so you know what you are doing when igniting it in cramped and flammable quarters. Always leave the tent door open during the operation. Ventilation is desirable, and if the stove starts spewing flaming gasoline and you can't shut it off, throw it out in the snow.

Propane stoves are less likely to flare up, as the fuel is already vaporized before it gets to the burner and ignites immediately. It is possible to fill the tent full of fumes if the valve is opened before the matches are ready, which could create an explosion and fire. In extremely cold temperatures compressed gas may vaporize slowly and not put out much heat. Be sure not to set the bottle or cartridge directly on snow. One way to warm the cartridge is to set it in a cooking pot so heat from the burner is reflected toward the cartridge and retained around it. Kerosene is less dangerous, but no less damaging if spilled fuel is ignited. Lighter fluid makes the safest priming fluid, as it is much less volatile than white gas and comes in spill-proof cans with accurate pouring spouts; alcohol is also good. Liquid kerosene doesn't burn with a hot enough flame to preheat the burner. If the burner has not been heated enough, the flame is sickly yellow with lots of smoke. Often the priming cup must be filled twice to adequately heat the burner. When preheated adequately, kerosene burns with a clean blue flame. Use a piece of fireproof foam material as a stove base, for all three fuels, so the stove does not come in contact with the tent floor and possibly melt it.

No matter what type of stove is used, be wide awake and alert before lighting it. Make sure you have a "pricker" to clean the burner orifice if it carbons up and plugs, no matter what type of fuel is used. Be very careful to keep dirt out of stoves which must be dismantled for carrying. Check pump leathers and gaskets frequently, as they do need to be replaced occasionally.

A large stable stove that has a larger burner to melt quantities of snow rapidly has advantages, but being large, it will be heavy. This category includes most of the kerosene-burning models, and some gas ones, which fold quickly into protective metal cases. Most kerosene models must be dismantled for carrying, but weigh less than the folding stoves which often have a very heavy case.

Some small, very lightweight stoves have very large burners and will put out a great deal of heat for their size. Although a nuisance, it will save weight to merely refill the small stove oftener than the large one with a large capacity fuel tank. A large stove may melt as much snow as two small ones, and weigh as much (which comes out even in cooking efficiency) but it will support a container three times as large with less danger of spillage than a smaller one. There are proponents of both large, heavy and stable, and small, light and unstable stoves loose in the hills and no attempt will be made here to arbitrate the problem.

The greatest problem in tent housekeeping is melting snow for water. A large pot is necessary to hold the large volume of snow. Potential disasters develop when a gallon of water is perched on top of a 1/2 pint stove, especially when the ingredients for dinner have been added. Dumping snow in the pot usually leaves some dribbles of snow from the tent door to, and around, the pot on the stove. Dipping hot water from the container adds more drops to the tent floor. If the stove is set on the floor without an insulating pad or piece of plywood under it, melting of the snow underneath may let it slowly tip the water pot off the burner. A little care and preparation will do wonders in successfully preparing food in the shelter.

Certain techniques are learned when cooking over a small stove in cramped quarters. Limited heat on a single burner dictates that one course be prepared and consumed at a time. The time and bother in melting snow for water generally prompts people to choose a one-course, one-dish meal. In its simplest form, snow is melted, the water heated and poured into individual containers to re-constitute some dehydrated or freeze-dried food. More snow is added to the pot, and by the time the food is eaten, more hot water is available. If someone is still hungry, another round is fixed, and more snow added to the pot. As each person finishes eating, the hot water is used for cocoa, tea, powdered juice mix, or coffee to rinse the food residue from the cup.

The vast variety of dehydrated foods available since World War II has gained immense popularity. Replacing the traditional can of pork and beans, the new foods are lightweight, simple, and fast to reconstitute. Cost is quite high, especially when the items are packaged in individual servings. Directions must be read carefully, as some require only the addition of boiling water and others are best when added to some other ingredient. Still others must be soaked in one kettle and then fried; read the labels carefully at home to be sure to take along enough utensils.

Great progress has been made in saving weight, but despite the exotic names on the package, the flavor is uniformly drab and monotonous without additional seasoning. Backpackers have little choice, as the alternatives are prohibitive weight or starvation. Snowshoers have an option; cold temperatures and availability of snow for refrigeration make it possible to include uncooked meat, frozen foods, and other perishables in the menu. However the weight of these items is so great they will only be used as a delicious respite from the processed mainstay.

Encourage ingenuity in menu planning. Mountain snowshoers have revolutionized snowshoe design and technique—it's about time someone did something about the food.

Garbage and Waste

The snow cover which transforms the landscape is temporary. It is easy to forget that the blanket which covers all ugliness will melt away and reveal every tin can and candy wrapper left by thoughtless winter campers. The message is brief and admits no exceptions: if you can carry it in full, you can carry it out empty.

Human wastes cannot be buried in topsoil as they should be in summer, so choose as unobtrusive a location as possible, such as the depths of a clump of trees, and, whenever possible, burn the used toilet paper.

Chapter 13

MOUNTAIN RESCUE

Over the years people have become lost, injured and/or been killed in the mountains and backcountry, and so a chain of responsibility has developed to organize and put into action certain search and rescue procedures. In Washington State the county sheriffs have been delegated this authority, although certain areas, such as National Parks and Indian reservations have their own organization completely independent of State or local control.

As no one has really wanted this responsibility, there is no uniform method of determining how such matters should be handled. In general the sheriff's personnel are not trained for searching the woods and hills for lost people or bringing climbers off high peaks, so they have used volunteers such as the various Mountain Rescue units, Civil Air Patrol, U.S. Forest Service rangers, and jeep clubs, and recently have helped sponsor Scout Explorer Search and Rescue groups. In some National Parks rangers do this type of work with outside volunteers called in to aid the park rescue team.

The traditional method of obtaining help in a backcountry emergency is to get word to the local sheriff (or to a ranger if in a National Park). The sheriff then evaluates the problem and starts organizing the search or rescue. This may involve getting medical aid, calling for volunteers to bring the person out, arranging for a helicopter, setting up an air search, bringing in a canine search group, or a combination of methods. State Civil Defense usually helps coordinate efforts, especially if several State and federal agencies are contributing to the operation. For large searches several branches of the military may be involved, utilizing Air Force, Army, and Navy helicopters as well as Civil Air Patrol.

The helicopter has become the real backbone of backcountry rescue, taking a load off the foot-propelled rescuer. The availability of helicopters from MAST — Military Aid for Safety and Traffic — may be variable, depending on military involvement elsewhere. Occasionally Coast Guard choppers are also available. Performance has been improved so much since the 1950s that injured climbers have been lifted off Mt. McKinley at over 17,000 feet and Mountain Rescue people flown to 14,000 feet on Mt. Rainier, then picked up again.

Winter snow closes many access roads, and complicates search and rescue. Bad weather is likely to be a factor, too, hampering the use of helicopters and light planes. In fact, just about every wheel- and foot-propelled search group is stalled on the steps of the Sheriff's office. A 10-mile round trip in rough country in average snow conditions can be considered a strenuous day on snowshoes, illustrating how deep snow isolates the backcountry. A rescue party on foot will need to carry overnight gear, and set up an advance base camp just to get to the backcountry; instead of a quick dash up a trail to the location of the problem, the winter rescue is going to last several days to accomplish anything. Obviously people on foot are frequently not able to get to the victim soon enough. Snowmobiles have a good potential for increasing the range of a search party, but the machines move too fast for thorough search and are limited almost entirely to roads. Foot-powered rescuers may have an aversion to snow machines and few snowmobilers have any experience in searching, let alone snowshoeing. A combination of methods is usually the solution.

In November 1971 jeeps and snowmobiles were used to transport Tacoma Mountain Rescue people and a German Shepherd Search Group to Corral Pass, north of Mt. Rainier to search for a hunter who had been missing overnight. By getting to the area where the victim was supposed to be more quickly and easily, the foot searchers were able to search strenuously and effectively. The hunter was located, and although he was disoriented and somewhat incoherent, he walked out on his own power after being warmed with hot drinks.

In December of the same year a similar situation occurred east of Blewett Pass on U.S. 97 in the east central Washington Cascades. Another hunter was missing in temperatures of about 10°F. The sheriff called in Ellensburg Mountain Rescue and Snowmobile Search and Rescue personnel and a search was begun about 11:00 P.M. on snowmobiles. They were successful in locating the missing man's trail, although it entered country too rugged to follow on machines. It was clear that the victim must be followed on foot, and two men did so, while snowmobiles patrolled roads on the edges of the area. The search was completed when the hunter walked out the next afternoon, with the foot searchers only about a half hour behind him.

Usually there is little demand for great numbers of searchers or mountain rescue people in winter. Hunters may create problems, especially when special hunts in high areas last until December 31. Poor visibility due to clouds and storm, short days and difficult traveling are sufficient to trap some. Others, on a blood trail from a wounded animal, would rather spend a night out than give up a possible trophy.

As more and more people go out in the hills for winter recreation, it is logical to assume that from time to time they will find themselves in need of outside help. Summer rescue techniques will work in winter except for the added problem of snow-covered access roads which make it difficult to rapidly get to the area where the problem is.

Aircraft are another object of winter searches, and several are lost during storms in the Cascades each year. Unfortunately their range is so great that only other aircraft can search for them effectively. To send out ground parties to look for a missing light plane that left Yakima and did not arrive in Seattle 100 miles away is unrealistic. Planes are usually the victims of bad weather and this in turn prevents any immediate air search, and so at times authorities solicit foot-powered volunteers to search an area in the faint hope that they will stumble onto the wreckage.

In 1970 and 1971 Ellensburg Mountain Rescue sponsored Washington Mountain Rescue Winter Training Conferences. A great deal more work must be done to solve problems, but several conclusions may already be drawn: no single rescue organization is adequate to handle a problem 5 to 10 miles from a road in winter. People on snowshoes and skis are too limited in range to move quickly enough. If they must carry overnight equipment and food for several days, their speed and range are further curtailed. Add to this the general lack of enthusiasm of trained rescue personnel for winter outings and the result is a greatly reduced number of people available for such problems.

Winter training programs, spending at least one night in a snow camp, have not been overattended. Some inquiries were received by the conference personnel about the accomodations at the motel convention center. However, it was the sponsoring snowshoers' philosophy that effective training duplicates the actual rescue experience. If you are going to meet and just sit and talk, you don't need all that time. Winter demands a great deal of searchers which only experience or training sessions in winter can provide.

People who frequent the winter backcountry need to be the basis for improving present backcountry rescue groups. It is good insurance to be an active participant in a functioning group which can get out and move, and help anyone in trouble in the winter hills. I've limped out after being somewhat mistreated by sliding snow, and a number of other people have had even narrower escapes than that. There is no better motivation than knowing the rescue group you are helping to train may someday come and get you out of trouble.

Again, preparation is invaluable. In case of accident, what are you going to do if you need outside help? First, of course, objectively evaluate the situation—don't waste time analyzing the cause. If the problem

Looking west from the slopes of Liberty Bell Peak at Washington Pass.

is an injury, care for the victim and get help. Consider alternative routes out to a road, if any exist. If you need help quickly and there is a good shortcut out to a road, go, and later figure out how to get back to your car.

Do give some thought and time to the subject of winter rescue. If you are asked to participate in such an operation, consider it an honor. Sometimes, in our impersonal and affluent society, one has the impression that no one needs a helping hand. But if someone is in trouble in the mountains in winter, he needs help, and may need it desperately.

Chapter 14

WHERE TO SNOWSHOE

Outdoor people near the Cascades, Sierras, and Rockies enjoy their mountains all year. Mountain and backcountry areas are usually open to anyone who wants to use them. A good part of the land is public, and is under the authority of the U.S. Forest Service, U.S. Park Service, or other federal agencies. Most States have similar agencies, such as the Department of Natural Resources in Washington State. The Washington State Department of Game also manages large blocks of land as game ranges. The agencies and departments continue on down to State, county, and city parks. Few of these agencies except the National Parks have restrictions on foot travel on land within their jurisdiction. National Parks are prime scenic country, with many trails through high mountains and deep valleys; when snow covered such areas present greater hazards than less scenic areas, and thus there are more restrictions on their use. Mt. Rainier, for example, experiences very heavy snowfall; over 1200 inches were recorded during the winter of 1971-72, a world record (this is the total of all fresh snowfalls, not the total on the ground at once).

Recreational use of National Park and National Forest lands is encouraged; ranger districts within the many separate National Forests print pamphlets and snowtrail maps for snowmobilers, snowshoers, and skiers. So far only the snowmobile trails have markers on the actual routes.

Other agencies are prepared to a lesser degree for snowshoers. Private landowners include a few notable exceptions to the "Welcome

Snowshoers" theme. Check with the owner before entering private land. Ski areas do not encourage snowshoers, who take up valuable parking space and do not leave the type of trail downhill skiers appreciate. White Pass and Mission Ridge do, however, cater to snowshoers who want to ride the lifts up and continue on to the backcountry beyond. Usually snowshoers in groups must arrive a half hour before opening time to ride the chair lifts so they will not interfere with the skiers. Check by phone or personally to arrange for parking and use of the lift.

In addition to covering the debris careless people scatter as they motor from downtown to picnic and hiking areas, snow covers a lot of roads. Generally all the backroads in the snow belt are closed in winter, with only the main highways plowed. On cross-Cascade routes the authorities restrict roadside parking and refrain from plowing any parking areas, thus denying the snowshoer the best close access to mountain and backcountry in Washington. During storms this rule is enforced rigidly because the plows can hardly keep up with the falling snow and cars parked on the road shoulder impede their work. When they get caught up they do plow out a few parking places. Check with snowplow operators and State Patrol; they sometimes can fit a car or two into a niche only they know about. Snowmobiles must be licensed in Washington, and part of these funds are used to plow parking areas primarily for this group of users. However, these places are not reserved exclusively for snowmobilers.

Generally country roads with light traffic, State routes that deadend back in the hills, or the approaches to mountain passes closed by snow in the winter are better bets for parking. The rule of the road is to park on the right hand side with your vehicle pointed in the direction of travel. If the road deadends, turn around and park on the right side headed back. Don't block the turnaround.

Generally people on snowshoes want to extend the summer outdoor experience and seek the type of terrain in winter that they enjoy during summer. Winter hikers generally must move to the next lower elevation, and mountain climbers find that peaks they would consider second-rate in summer are about all they can handle in winter. Trail hikers find logging roads in winter to be about the same difficulty as the summer trail. The meadow walkers hardly need to leave town, except that a mountain meadow has so much lovelier a setting than does a city park. Snow-covered sagebrush hills in the west can be amazingly attractive for snowshoeing during the rather brief periods of snowcover.

Each area is different. Some summer dude ranches are in very fine snowshoeing country and encourage winter use of their facilities, one of which is parking space. There is some conflict with snowmobiles on snow-covered logging roads. Some people do not care to walk where others ride. The machines do break out a good trail, which is at times firm enough to walk on without snowshoes. Usually, however, these

Mt. Mastiff, north of US 2, east of Stevens Pass.

machines cannot negotiate hillsides and so are more common on first rate logging roads, leaving the high country limited to foot travel.

Snowshoers often will have to find trips on their own, as this is a fairly new activity and guidebooks are scarce or nonexistent for most areas. The best thing to do is to pioneer and find your own winter trails and scenic places. You may find places that are perfect for snowshoeing and totally unused by anyone else.

The fact that winter makes the outdoors so much more rugged can be an advantage. You may not need to drive long distances to find a rewarding walk. A farmer's field may be just right for an afternoon snowshoe hike with the children, or a walk along a local creek may provide a setting you never suspected existed.

It isn't entirely the scenery that makes snowshoeing so delightful. Part of it is the peace and serenity of the snow-covered land around. It may be physically punishing, yet emotionally exhilarating. A minimum of skill can provide a whole new world of outdoor experience. Attitude is vital to the enjoyment of the winter outdoors. No one expects to get a free ride on snowshoes, which helps create a spirit of friendliness among a party of snowshoers.

You feel a sense of awe at the beauty and immensity of the natural world. There is contrast with the disorder, congestion, harsh noises and ugliness of the urban sprawl. Snow cover gives the impression of rounded forms rather than harsh lines. The natural soundproofing of snow mutes loud noises and you can sense a calmness which is soothing to shattered nerves.

There is a feeling of personal insignificance standing on a high point with ridge after ridge extending to the horizon and a sharp peak or massive volcano dominating everything else. Man's efforts at creativity simply cannot compare with the natural scene. You may feel a deeper appreciation for the power of natural forces, not just the violence of storm and avalanche, but also the quiet Being who must have clad a thousand hills in forest, and added snow each winter to nourish the rivers and give the land a rest.

We are strangers in an alien land; man doesn't belong in the winter wilderness. The mountain landscape speaks visually through its beauty and the silence of calm days of eternity, in contrast to people who are short-lived visitors. The roar of the storm does not dim the grandeur, but emphasizes that man must tread gently and with the utmost care. A gust of windblown snow and man and his snowshoe trail are gone.

God left His presence in the winter mountains. We should honor Him by leaving the snowy hills unmarred by our careless actions so they may awe others. God's ways are above man's ways, but as long as I am permitted, I will take this passage literally, and lift up my eyes—and my body as well—unto the hills, from whence cometh my help. (Psalms 121:1)

Mt. Stuart from Ingalls Lake.

APPENDIX

APPENDIX

EQUIPMENT CHECKLIST

Many of the items in this list have not needed description in the text. By the time they are ready to try snowshoeing, most people have acquired some knowledge and equipment, and general suggestions should be adequate. If any doubt remains, further reference material can be found in the Suggested Reading List.

The following checklist is not intended to be definitive. Other items may be equally satisfactory; the last word on snowshoeing equipment has yet to be written. Try your own ideas, improvise, and modify. There is plenty of room for improvement.

Not all items need be taken on all trips. On an easy, short hike some items may be excluded. For longer hikes where a delay could force an overnight stay, start adding the items listed under Group and Optional.

Snowshoe groups usually stay together because the stronger members cannot outrun the weaker when breaking trail through deep snow. A tired person cannot be left to sit beside the trail several hours in 10°F weather so that the rest of the party can continue to the objective. Therefore some items such as map and compass may be shared within a group, and to a lesser extent, first aid supplies. Make sure someone has the items you plan to leave home. Experienced people inadvertently overlook items such as matches at times. Make sure these items are within the party before you start walking.

Ski poles fully occupy both hands, and even with an ice ax, a headlight type flashlight is more practical than a hand held one. Headlights which use a 6 volt battery give much longer service than 2-cell models and are strongly recommended. Cold temperature shortens battery life and short days require more flashlight use, so equip yourself better than in summer.

Add a stove per group for a hot drink during rest stop. Don't skimp on matches and fire starter if you intend to build a fire; remember dry wood is scarce or nonexistent at this time of year. Carry a knife with a leather punch and add the saw to group equipment. Shovel and snow saw are optional and depend on the length of the trip and risk of an overnight stay on one-day trips.

Extra food is of less importance because the risk of starvation during an overnight stay is slight, but the risk of hypothermia and/or frostbite is very high if you are caught in a storm without much shelter. Most of the small emergency kits contain a tea bag, bouillion and sugar cubes as extra food. These items won't do much to prolong life; their chief purpose is to help pass the unpleasant hours more easily and to improve the taste of wood-ash-flavored melted snow.

As you gain experience from snowshoeing in different conditions, deciding what to put in your pack will be less of a problem. Some equipment desirable on a sub-zero temperature outing will not be necessary for a mid-May, 60°F hike. If there are beginners along, be sure to check that everyone has the essentials; take the time and effort to help the first-timer shake down his equipment.

Plan your equipment creatively and don't depend blindly on what any checklist indicates. Improvise and experiment so that your equipment will meet the varying conditions you find in the mountains without unnecessary fussing and adjusting. If the gear you have doesn't work, learn to make it work or replace it. Don't spend your outdoor time changing clothes and tightening or loosening straps and buckles. Enjoy the winter hills to the fullest while you are there.

ONE-DAY HIKE
Clothing

Underwear
Wool shirt, with or without T-shirt or long sleeve jersey
Wool pants with tie-down or gaiters, expedition overboots or mukluks
Wind pants or warm ups—preferably with leg zippers
Down or fiberfill parka, or down vest and dacron-filled parka
Wool cap and face mask or combination
Wool mitts and extras, or overmitts, ski mitts or snowmobile mitts
Wool socks, cotton next to skin if necessary

Climbing or hiking boots or insulated boots of foam rubber; felt
   liners if necessary

Add for extra warmth if needed
   Quilted down or dacron - filled jacket or sweater
   Scarf

Equipment

Snowshoes, bindings, and traction device
Ice ax with basket or ski poles
Frame pack or rucksack
Sun goggles, sun cream
Matches and fire starter
First aid kit containing bandages, tape, moleskin or adhesive foam,
   scissors, bandages
Repair cord and pocket knife with leather punch
Flashlight, preferably headlight type
Canteen or thermos
Lunch and a little extra food
Toilet paper

Add, per group
   Compass and map of the area—1 or 2
   Flagging—plastic or crepe paper
   Folding saw—1
   Snow saw or shovel for creek crossings, etc.—1
   Wands with flagging attached—25 (if route is intricate or long)
   Plastic or nylon tarps—1 or 2 (for emergency overnight stay)

If weather is 10°F or colder, add, or change to
   Extra warm clothing
   Insulated warm ups or long underwear and wind pants
   Down mitts or especially warm insulated mitts
   Expedition overboots over heavy climbing or double boots
   Sweater—wool, down or dacron
   Stove and pot for hot drinks or heavy duty fire starter

OVERNIGHT TRIPS

Extra socks and mitts
Snorkel—optional
Down - filled tent slippers—optional
Adequate sleeping bag
Foam pad
Cup, spoon and cooking utensils as needed
Hot breakfast and dinners, with hot drink
Cold lunch; optional—stop to heat water for hot drink on trail

For the group
    Tent or tents—adequate space for entire group
    Snow anchors
    Rainfly—optional
    Plastic or nylon tarp or large garbage sack for storing packs
      and gear outside if there is not enough room in tents
    Stove, extra fuel, large enough pot to melt snow
    Base for stove or metal fire platform
    Shovel, snow saw for leveling tent platform or digging cave or
      building igloo
    Whisk broom to brush snow off boots, etc., brought into tent

SUGGESTED READING LIST

Fear, Gene. **Surviving the Unexpected Wilderness Emergency.** Tacoma, Washington: Survival Education Association, 1972.

Ferber, Peggy, ed. **Mountaineering: The Freedom of the Hills** (3rd edition). Seattle, Washington: The Mountaineers, 1974.

LaChapelle, Edward R. **The ABC of Avalanche Safety.** Denver, Colorado: Colorado Outdoor Sports Co., 1970

Manning, Harvey. **Backpacking: One Step at a Time.** Seattle, Washington: Recreational Equipment, Inc., 1972.

Mitchell, Dick. **Mountaineering First Aid.** Seattle, Washington: The Mountaineers, 1972.

OTHER BOOKS
FROM THE MOUNTAINEERS

Mountaineering: The Freedom of the Hills
Textbook for the Mountaineers Climbing Course, the new Third Edition carries on the tradition of being the standard in its field. Technical rock and ice climbing techniques and equipment updated, as well as first aid, rescue, and information on camping and hiking. Profusely illustrated with line drawings and photographs. 478 pages, 6" x 9", hardbound.

The Alpine Lakes
Superb, full-color presentation on the wilderness heart of Washington's Cascade Mounains. Ed Cooper and Bob Gunning, in 95 outstanding color photos, portray the area's mountains, forest trails, tarns, snowfields, granite cliffs. Text describes personal experiences in exploring the Alpine Lakes. 128 pages, 10" x 13 1/2", hardbound.

Cascade Alpine Guide
Climbing and High Routes: Columbia River to Stevens Pass. First completely detailed climbing guide to the south Cascades; prepared by Fred Beckey. Includes extensive route coverage, plus approach - route material, data on Cascade geology, weather, and natural history. Over 100 pages of maps, sketches; photos with routes overprinted in red. 354 pages, 7" x 8 1/2", flexible binding.

Climber's Guide to the Olympic Mountains

Covers every climbing and approach route on the Olympic peaks; also high alpine traverses, ski and snowshoe tours. Prepared by Olympic Mountain Rescue. 240 pages, 9 maps, 17 peak sketches with routes; flexible binding.

Routes and Rocks

Hiker's Guide to the North Cascades from Glacier Peak to Lake Chelan. Detailed description of trails, off-trail high routes; with point-to-point mileages, elevations, campsites, notes on geology. By D.F. Crowder and R.W. Tabor, U.S.G.S. Plus three modified U.S.G.S. quad maps with overprint for routes, 240 pages, hardbound.

The Challenge of Rainier

Dee Molenaar's complete documentation of the climbing history of Mount Rainier, from the discovery years and the pioneering efforts to today's climbing parties. Personal anecdotes and word-portraits of guides through the various eras. Sketches, more than 100 photos, 7" x 10", hardbound.

Wildflowers of Mount Rainier and the Cascades

More than 100 full-color photos by Bob and Ira Spring of wildflowers, common and rare; authoritative text by Mary Fries. 220 pages, 7" x 8 1/2", hardbound.

Medicine for Mountaineering

Handbook for treating accidents, illnesses in remote areas. Compiled by climber-physicians, includes treatment of traumatic, enviromental injuries; emphasizes high-altitude illnesses. 350 pages, 100 drawings, hardbound.

Mountaineering First Aid

A guide to accident response and first aid care; helpful for dealing with remote-area accidents, and preventing them. Excellent added text for outdoor safety, first aid classes. 96 pages, paperbound.

In the Hikes Series:

All detailed guides to trail or road-and-trail hikes, with complete descriptions, sketch maps, and scenic photos for each. Volumes are 7" x 8 1/2", paperbound, approximately 200 pages each.

101 Hikes in the North Cascades

102 Hikes in the Alpine Lakes, South Cascades and Olympics

50 Hikes in Mount Rainier National Park

Trips and Trails, 1: Family Camps, Short Hikes and View Roads in the North Cascades and Olympics

Trips and Trails, 2: Family Camps, Short Hikes and View Roads in the South Cascades and Mt. Rainier

Footloose Around Puget Sound: 100 Walks on Beaches, Lowlands and Foothills

55 Ways to the Wilderness in Southcentral Alaska

103 Hikes in Southwestern British Columbia

Bicycling the Backroads Around Puget Sound